FAITHFUL ACROSS GENERATIONS

A Biblical Vision for Leadership, Legacy, and Mission

Dr. K. A. *"Shawn"* Dooley

ACKNOWLEDGMENTS 6

PREFACE 8

FOREWORD 10

INTRODUCTION 12

CHAPTER 1 14

THE GENERATIONAL LEADERSHIP GAP: A MINISTRY AND MISSIONAL CRISIS 14

SECTION 1 14
WHAT THE GENERATIONAL LEADERSHIP GAP ACTUALLY LOOKS LIKE IN REAL CHURCHES 14
SECTION 2 18
WHY THE GAP PERSISTS EVEN IN FAITHFUL AND HEALTHY CHURCHES 18
SECTION 3 21
WHEN LEADERSHIP GAPS BECOME MISSIONAL LIABILITIES 21
SECTION 4 25
A BIBLICAL VISION OF LEADERSHIP ACROSS GENERATIONS 25
SECTION 5 29
FROM OWNERSHIP TO STEWARDSHIP: REFRAMING HOW THE CHURCH UNDERSTANDS LEADERSHIP 29
SECTION 6 32
A CALL TO COURAGEOUS AND FAITHFUL LEADERSHIP 32

CHAPTER 2 35

A BIBLICAL THEOLOGY OF GENERATIONAL LEADERSHIP 35

SECTION 1 35
LEADERSHIP WAS ALWAYS MEANT TO BE GENERATIONAL 35
SECTION 2 38
AUTHORITY, RESPONSIBILITY, AND THE SHARED NATURE OF LEADERSHIP 38
SECTION 3 41
MENTORSHIP, DISCIPLESHIP, AND THE POWER OF PROXIMITY 41
SECTION 4 44
LEADERSHIP FORMED IN COMMUNITY, NOT IN ISOLATION 44
SECTION 5 47
THE ROLE OF THE HOLY SPIRIT IN GENERATIONAL LEADERSHIP 47
SECTION 6 50
RECOVERING A FAITHFUL AND GENERATIONAL VISION OF LEADERSHIP 50

CHAPTER 3 52

WHY CHURCHES STRUGGLE TO CHANGE WHAT THEY CAN CLEARLY SEE 52

SECTION 1 52
WHEN THEOLOGY IS CLEAR, BUT PRACTICE IS COMPLICATED 52
SECTION 2 56
POWER, CONTROL, AND THE UNSPOKEN HIERARCHIES OF CHURCH LEADERSHIP 56
SECTION 3 60
WHEN THE FEAR OF DIVISION BECOMES A BARRIER TO FAITHFUL CHANGE 60
SECTION 4 63
WHEN AVOIDANCE BECOMES CULTURE AND CULTURE RESISTS CHANGE 63
SECTION 5 66
THE COURAGE TO NAME WHAT IS HOLDING THE CHURCH BACK 67

CHAPTER 4 70

FROM CALLING TO CAPACITY: BUILDING INTERGENERATIONAL LEADERSHIP PIPELINES 70

SECTION 1 70
WHY CHURCHES NEED PIPELINES, NOT JUST PASSION 70
SECTION 2 74
IDENTIFYING EMERGING LEADERS ACROSS GENERATIONS: FROM ASSUMPTION TO DISCERNMENT
.... 74
SECTION 3 77
DEVELOPING LEADERS THROUGH GRADUATED RESPONSIBILITY 77
SECTION 4 80
CREATING SAFE-TO-LEARN ENVIRONMENTS FOR EMERGING LEADERS 80
SECTION 5 83
INSTITUTIONALIZING LEADERSHIP DEVELOPMENT FOR LONG-TERM FAITHFULNESS 83
SECTION 6 86
FROM INTENTION TO INFRASTRUCTURE: PREPARING THE CHURCH FOR GENERATIONAL
CONTINUITY 86

CHAPTER 5 88

GENERATIONS IN DIALOGUE: MOVING FROM TENSION TO TRUST 88

SECTION 1 88
WHY STRUCTURES FAIL WITHOUT RELATIONSHIPS 88
SECTION 2 91
STORYTELLING AS A BRIDGE BETWEEN MEMORY AND VISION 91
SECTION 3 94
LISTENING AS A DISCIPLINE THAT SUSTAINS INTERGENERATIONAL LEADERSHIP 94
SECTION 4 97
FROM CONVERSATION TO COLLABORATION: LEADING TOGETHER ACROSS GENERATIONS 97
SECTION 5 100
WHEN RELATIONSHIPS BECOME THE PATHWAY TO SHARED LEADERSHIP 100

CHAPTER 6 103

FROM CONTINUITY TO COMMISSION: GENERATIONAL LEADERSHIP AND THE MISSION OF THE CHURCH 103

> SECTION 1 103
> WHY GENERATIONAL LEADERSHIP IS A MISSIONAL ISSUE, NOT AN INTERNAL ONE 103
> SECTION 2 106
> HOW INTERGENERATIONAL LEADERSHIP STRENGTHENS DISCIPLESHIP AND OUTREACH 106
> SECTION 3 108
> PREPARING THE CHURCH FOR A CHANGING WORLD THROUGH GENERATIONAL LEADERSHIP .. 108
> SECTION 4 111
> GENERATIONAL LEADERSHIP AND THE CHURCH'S ENDURING WITNESS 111
> SECTION 5 113
> LEADERSHIP RENEWAL AS AN ACT OF MISSIONAL FAITHFULNESS 113

CHAPTER 7 116

FAITHFUL STEWARDS OF WHAT WE HAVE RECEIVED 116

> SECTION 1 116
> STANDING AT THE THRESHOLD OF GENERATIONAL RESPONSIBILITY 116
> SECTION 2 119
> COMMITMENTS THAT TURN CONVICTION INTO FAITHFUL ACTION 119
> SECTION 3 121
> THE COURAGE TO RELEASE WHAT GOD NEVER INTENDED US TO KEEP 121
> SECTION 4 125
> REMAINING PRESENT WITHOUT STANDING IN THE WAY 125
> SECTION 5 128
> A COMMISSION TO LEAD FAITHFULLY ACROSS GENERATIONS 128

ABOUT THE AUTHOR 130

FAITHFUL ACROSS GENERATIONS 131

CHURCH & LEADERSHIP STUDY GUIDE 131

Copyright © 2025 by Dr. K. A. "Shawn" Dooley

All rights reserved.

No part of this book may be reproduced, stored in a retrieval system, or transmitted in any form or by any means electronic, mechanical, photocopying, recording, or otherwise without prior written permission
of the publisher, except for brief quotations in reviews.

Scripture quotations are taken from the Holy Bible,
King James Version (KJV), public domain.

This book is a work of non-fiction. While based on real ministry and pastoral experience, all names of churches and identifying details have been omitted or altered to protect confidentiality.

ISBN: 9798241220202

Printed in the United States of America

First Edition

Acknowledgments

This book exists because I did not walk this journey alone. Like the very message it carries, *Faithful Across Generations* is the result of relationships, mentorship, patience, and trust that have been stewarded over time.

First and foremost, I give thanks to God, whose faithfulness extends from generation to generation. Every season of ministry, study, and leadership reflected in these pages is evidence of His grace, guidance, and sustaining power. This work is ultimately an offering back to Him.

I am deeply grateful to the leader's pastors, mentors, professors, and ministry elders who invested in me long before I understood the weight of leadership. Your wisdom, correction, encouragement, and example shaped not only my theology, but my posture toward ministry and stewardship. You modeled what it looks like to lead faithfully while preparing others to do the same.

To the congregations and ministry contexts that allowed me to learn, grow, wrestle, and lead thank you. Much of what is written here was formed through real conversations, real tension, real prayer, and real trust. Your willingness to walk through seasons of growth and transition helped clarify the convictions expressed in this book.

I am especially thankful for emerging leaders who continue to inspire this work. Your questions, passion, and desire to serve remind me that leadership development is not a theoretical exercise, but a sacred responsibility. You are not interruptions to the church's story you are part of its continuation.
To my family, thank you for your patience, support, and understanding throughout the long hours of study, writing, and ministry. Your encouragement sustained me more than you know.

Finally, I acknowledge every reader who loves the church enough to wrestle with difficult questions and trust God enough to prepare others to lead. If this book helps even one leader steward faith more faithfully across generations, it has fulfilled its purpose.

Preface

Why I Wrote This Book
This book was born out of both conviction and concern.
Over the years, I have had countless conversations with pastors, ministry leaders, and church members who love the church deeply but sense a growing tension beneath the surface. The tension is not always loud or confrontational. Often, it is quiet expressed in unspoken expectations, delayed conversations, and uncertainty about the future.

I have witnessed churches rich in history and faithfulness struggle to prepare leaders beyond the present moment. I have seen dedicated leaders carry responsibility faithfully while feeling unsure how or when to entrust others. I have also encountered emerging leaders eager to serve but uncertain where they fit or how their calling will be nurtured.

What became increasingly clear is that many of these challenges were not rooted in a lack of faith or commitment. They were rooted in how leadership was understood and practiced.
This book grew out of my doctoral work, but it is not written for academic debate alone. It is written from within the life of the church, shaped by pastoral ministry, leadership development, and real congregational experience. The questions explored here are not theoretical they are lived.

I wrote *Faithful Across Generations* because I believe the church is strongest when leadership is stewarded rather than preserved, shared rather than guarded, and entrusted rather than assumed. I believe Scripture offers a compelling vision of leadership that spans generations, honors faithfulness, and prepares the people of God for continued mission.

This book is not written to criticize churches or leaders. It is written to encourage reflection, courage, and obedience. My hope is that readers will not simply gain insight, but develop posture one marked by humility, trust, and confidence in God's ongoing work.

If this book helps leaders ask better questions, listen more deeply, invest more intentionally, and release more faithfully, then it has served its purpose.

May God use these pages to strengthen His church not just for today, but for generations to come.

FOREWORD
From Dr. W.G. "Will" Jackson II

Faithfulness That Reaches Forward
Every generation of the church faces the same sacred question, though it often sounds different in each season: Will we be faithful only to what we have received, or also to those who will come after us?

In *Faithful Across Generations*, Dr. K. A. "Shawn" Dooley invites the church to confront that question with theological clarity, pastoral honesty, and practical wisdom. This book is not driven by anxiety about decline, nor by fascination with novelty. Instead, it is grounded in a deeper conviction that faithfulness is inherently generational and that leadership in the church is always an act of stewardship.

What makes this work especially timely is its refusal to treat generational leadership as merely a technical or organizational problem. Many books address succession planning, leadership pipelines, or generational differences. Far fewer ask the more demanding theological questions: *What does Scripture say about leadership being entrusted? How does power shape formation? Why do churches resist change even when theology is clear? And what does faithfulness require of leaders when their season begins to shift?*

Dr. Dooley writes as both pastor and theologian one who understands the complexity of congregational life and the weight leaders carry. His analysis is honest without being cynical, challenging without being dismissive. He names fear, control, silence, and conflict avoidance not to condemn the church, but to call it back to courage and trust in God's ongoing work.
Perhaps most importantly, this book insists that generational leadership is not about replacement, competition, or loss. It is about obedience. It is about forming leaders before crisis demands it, cultivating trust across difference, and releasing authority as an act of worship rather than retreat. In a cultural moment marked by polarization, impatience, and fragmentation, this vision is both countercultural and deeply biblical.

Pastors will find in these pages language for conversations they have long sensed but struggled to articulate. Church leaders will discover frameworks that are practical without being simplistic. Students and scholars will appreciate the theological grounding that gives this work durability beyond trends and techniques.

Faithful Across Generations reminds us that the church does not belong to any one leader, era, or generation. It belongs to God. And the same God who was faithful to those before us will remain faithful to those who come after if we have the courage to entrust what we have received.

This book is a gift to the church, and more importantly, it is an invitation to lead with humility, to steward with wisdom, and to believe that God's work across generations is far from finished.

Introduction

Faithfulness Is Not Automatic
Every church believes it is being faithful. Worship services continue, ministries function, and leaders labor week after week to serve God's people. Faithfulness is assumed because activity is visible. Yet Scripture reminds us that faithfulness is not measured by motion alone, it is revealed through obedience over time.

What many churches rarely stop to ask is not whether they are faithful in the present, but whether that faithfulness is being stewarded for the future.

Across denominations and traditions, congregations are filled with devoted leaders who have prayed, sacrificed, and served for years. Their labor has sustained the church through seasons of growth, decline, transition, and renewal. At the same time, a quieter question often lingers beneath the surface: Who is being prepared to lead next and how?

This book was written because faith is rarely lost all at once. More often, it fades slowly. It fades when leadership is protected rather than entrusted, when authority is held but not shared, and when generations worship in the same space but rarely lead together. The issue is not a lack of commitment or sincerity. The issue is stewardship.

Scripture presents faithfulness as generational by design. God identifies Himself through generations, revealing His covenantal faithfulness from Abraham to Isaac to Jacob. The people of God are commanded not only to obey, but to teach, model, and pass on what they have received. The gospel is transmitted through relationship, formation, and trust. Leadership, therefore, was never intended to terminate with one generation it was always meant to be entrusted forward.
Yet for many churches, leadership transition is approached with anxiety rather than confidence. Fear of change, concern over loss of control, unresolved conflict, and unspoken assumptions often shape

leadership culture more than theology does. As a result, churches may remain active while becoming increasingly fragile, dependent on a small group of leaders with limited pathways for renewal.

Faithful Across Generations is not a critique of tradition, nor is it a call to reckless change. It is an invitation to recover a biblical vision of leadership as stewardship. It challenges churches to see authority not as possession, but as trust; leadership not as permanence, but as responsibility; and transition not as failure, but as obedience.

This book is written for pastors who carry the weight of leadership quietly, for ministry leaders navigating generational tension, and for emerging leaders discerning their calling within the church. It speaks to congregations that love their history and desire a faithful future, yet sense that intentional leadership formation must become a priority rather than an afterthought.

The chapters that follow will explore the theological foundations of generational leadership, name the cultural and relational barriers that hinder it, and offer practical pathways for developing leaders across generations. More importantly, this book invites readers to examine their own posture toward leadership, power, and trust in God's ongoing work.

Faithfulness is not automatic. It must be stewarded, practiced, and passed on. The future of the church depends not on preserving what has been, but on faithfully entrusting what God has given across generations.

CHAPTER 1
The Generational Leadership Gap: A Ministry and Missional Crisis

Section 1

What the Generational Leadership Gap Actually Looks Like in Real Churches

The generational leadership gap in the church rarely appears as open conflict. More often, it shows up quietly, embedded in routines, traditions, and long-standing assumptions about how leadership works. Churches do not typically announce that they are struggling with generational leadership; instead, the struggle becomes visible through patterns that repeat themselves year after year.

In many congregations, leadership meetings are populated by the same voices they have always been. Decisions are made faithfully, prayerfully, and with sincere concern for the church's well-being. Yet the composition of the room tells a story.

Younger adults may attend, but often as observers rather than contributors. Teenagers and young adults may serve in visible roles ushering, media, music, children's ministry but rarely participate in shaping vision, strategy, or direction.
This creates a leadership culture where participation is encouraged but influence is restricted.
Older leaders, many of whom have sacrificed deeply for the church, often carry a sense of responsibility that borders on guardianship. They have protected the church through seasons of hardship, change, and uncertainty. For them, leadership is not merely a role; it is a calling shaped by memory, struggle, and faithfulness. Releasing leadership, therefore, can feel like releasing identity.

Younger leaders, on the other hand, frequently carry a different burden. They desire to serve faithfully but struggle to understand where they fit beyond entry-level ministry roles. They attend leadership trainings, show initiative, and demonstrate competence, yet remain unsure whether their voice is truly welcome. Over time, enthusiasm gives way to hesitation. Initiative becomes silence. Silence eventually becomes disengagement.

What makes this dynamic especially challenging is that both generations often believe they are acting in the church's best interest.

Leadership Without a Pathway

One of the clearest indicators of a generational leadership gap is the absence of a defined leadership pathway. In many churches, leaders are identified informally rather than developed intentionally. Individuals step into roles because they are available, trusted, or have "always done it." While faithfulness is commendable, this approach often leaves emerging leaders without clarity about how growth happens.

When leadership pathways are unclear, several patterns emerge:
- Leadership transitions are delayed because no one feels "ready."
- Authority becomes attached to tenure rather than formation.
- Emerging leaders wait for permission that is never explicitly given.
- Senior leaders feel indispensable rather than supported.

In such environments, leadership succession becomes a looming crisis rather than a gradual process. Churches may recognize the need for transition but feel paralyzed by uncertainty, fearing that change will disrupt stability.

The Pastor as the Permanent Bridge

In churches with unresolved generational leadership gaps, the pastor often becomes the sole point of connection between generations. The pastor interprets concerns, mediates conflict, and translates expectations. While this role may be manageable in the short term, it is unsustainable in the long term.

Over time, the pastor absorbs pressure from both sides. Older leaders look to the pastor to preserve tradition and maintain order. Younger leaders look to the pastor to advocate for inclusion and opportunity. The pastor becomes the bridge, but without structural support, bridges eventually crack under the weight.

This dynamic also creates dependency. Instead of generations learning how to work together, they rely on the pastor to manage tension. Leadership development stalls because relationships are not allowed to mature organically across age groups.

Faithful Service Without Empowerment

Another hallmark of the generational leadership gap is the distinction between serving and leading. Many churches excel at mobilizing volunteers across generations yet struggle to empower leaders across generations.

Younger members are often encouraged to serve energetically, but leadership authority remains concentrated. This sends an unintended message: service is welcome, but leadership is reserved. Over time, this distinction shapes expectations and limits growth.

Leadership development requires more than opportunity, it requires trust, mentorship, and shared responsibility. Without these elements, churches unintentionally train younger generations to contribute labor without cultivating ownership.

A Crisis Hidden in Plain Sight

Because churches often remain functional while this gap exists, it can be easy to dismiss the issue as minor or temporary. Worship continues. Ministries operate. The church appears stable. Yet beneath this stability lies fragility.

When leadership is not intentionally transferred, churches become vulnerable during seasons of transition. Sudden illness, relocation, or retirement can expose the absence of prepared leaders. At that point, the issue is no longer theoretical, it becomes urgent.

The generational leadership gap is not a future problem; it is a present reality with future consequences.

Section Summary

This section has described how the generational leadership gap manifests in everyday church life not through rebellion or dysfunction, but through patterns of assumption, silence, and structural absence. Leadership without pathways, service without empowerment, and mediation without formation all contribute to a culture where generations coexist without true collaboration.

In the next section, we will explore why these patterns persist, even in churches that genuinely desire unity, growth, and faithfulness.

Section 2

Why the Gap Persists Even in Faithful and Healthy Churches

One of the most perplexing realities of the generational leadership gap is that it often exists in churches that are otherwise healthy. These are congregations that love Scripture, value prayer, support missions, and remain committed to their communities. The presence of a generational divide does not automatically signal theological compromise or spiritual neglect. In many cases, it emerges precisely because leaders are deeply invested in protecting what they believe God has built.
This is what makes the issue so complex. The gap does not persist because leaders do not care it persists because they care deeply, but often without shared clarity about how leadership is meant to be stewarded across time.

Faithfulness Without Formation

Many churches equate leadership readiness with longevity. Those who have served the longest are naturally trusted the most. Over time, faithfulness becomes the primary credential for authority. While faithfulness is a biblical virtue, it was never intended to function as the sole criterion for leadership continuity.

When faithfulness is not paired with formation, churches inadvertently reward endurance without preparing successors. Leadership roles remain occupied not because leaders are unwilling to train others, but because no structured process exists to move responsibility gradually and intentionally.

As a result, leadership transitions become emotionally charged moments rather than natural progressions. Senior leaders feel pressure to remain in place "until someone is ready," while emerging leaders struggle to discern what readiness even looks like.

The Fear Beneath the Surface

Beneath much of the resistance to leadership transition lies fear rarely named, often spiritualized, but deeply human.
Older leaders may fear that releasing leadership means diminishing relevance, identity, or voice. For many, leadership has been intertwined with personal faith journeys, sacrifice, and perseverance through difficult seasons. Stepping aside can feel like being written out of the story they helped shape.

Younger leaders often carry a different fear the fear of being exposed, failing publicly, or being labeled disrespectful for asking questions or proposing change. Without clear mentoring relationships, leadership feels risky rather than formative.
When fear goes unaddressed, it becomes embedded in culture. Leaders protect what they know. Emerging leaders retreat to what feels safe. The gap widens not through hostility, but through caution.

Tradition as a Shield Rather Than a Gift

Tradition plays a vital role in shaping church identity. It carries memory, theology, and testimony. However, when tradition becomes defensive rather than instructive, it can unintentionally block leadership development.
In some churches, tradition is treated as fragile, something that must be guarded rather than shared. This posture limits generational participation, as younger leaders are often perceived as threats to continuity rather than partners in preservation.
Biblically, tradition was never meant to be hoarded. It was meant to be handed down, taught, and embodied. When churches fail to teach the *why* behind tradition, they risk losing both the tradition and the next generation.

The Absence of Shared Language

Another reason the generational gap persists is the lack of shared language around leadership development. Churches may agree that "we need more young leaders," but rarely define what leadership development actually entails.

Without common language, expectations remain vague:
- What does mentoring look like?
- When does authority transfer?
- How are mistakes handled?
- Who evaluates readiness?

In the absence of clarity, assumptions fill the gap. Senior leaders assume emerging leaders will "step up when ready." Emerging leaders assume they must wait to be invited. Neither side feels empowered to initiate change.

Organizational Drift and Inherited Structures

Many leadership challenges are not intentionally designed, they are inherited. Churches often operate within structures created for previous generations, assuming those structures will continue to function indefinitely.

As culture shifts, these structures lose effectiveness but remain unchanged out of habit or reverence. The result is organizational drift: systems that once served the mission now slow it.

Generational gaps widen when structures do not evolve to support collaboration, mentoring, and shared leadership. What was once a strength becomes a limitation.

Section Summary

This section has shown that the generational leadership gap persists not because of spiritual failure, but because of unexamined assumptions, unaddressed fear, and inherited systems. Faithfulness without formation, tradition without transmission, and leadership without language all contribute to a culture where continuity is assumed rather than cultivated.

In the next section, we will examine how this leadership gap becomes a missional problem, affecting not only internal health but the church's capacity to engage its community and fulfill its calling.

Section 3

When Leadership Gaps Become Missional Liabilities

The generational leadership gap does not remain confined to internal meetings or leadership structures. Left unaddressed, it eventually shapes how the church engages or fails to engage the world around it. What begins as an internal leadership challenge becomes a missional liability.

Churches exist not merely to preserve belief, but to embody and proclaim the gospel in changing contexts. Leadership development plays a central role in that task. When leadership is not shared and cultivated across generations, the church's capacity to interpret culture, respond creatively, and connect relationally with its community is diminished.

Mission suffers not because the message has changed, but because the messengers are disconnected from one another.

The Disconnect Between the Church and Its Community

Younger generations often serve as cultural bridges between the church and the surrounding world. They understand emerging communication patterns, social realities, and the questions people are actually asking. When these voices are absent from leadership, churches may remain faithful in doctrine but increasingly disconnected in practice.

This disconnect does not happen overnight. It develops gradually as churches continue to operate with leadership perspectives shaped by past contexts. Ministries that once thrived may struggle to adapt. Outreach strategies may rely on methods that no longer resonate. Evangelistic efforts may feel sincere but ineffective.

The problem is not a lack of passion for evangelism; it is a lack of intergenerational discernment.

When younger leaders are excluded from shaping mission, churches lose insight into how faith is experienced and questioned in contemporary culture. Conversely, when older leaders are excluded from mentoring younger leaders in mission, churches lose theological grounding and historical wisdom. Mission requires both.

Evangelism Without Continuity

Another consequence of generational leadership gaps is episodic evangelism. Churches may host events, revivals, or outreach programs, yet struggle to sustain long-term engagement. Without leadership continuity, evangelism becomes something the church *does* rather than something it *is*.
Leadership continuity ensures that mission is not tied to individuals, seasons, or personalities. When leadership development is intentional, evangelism becomes embedded in culture. When it is not, mission fluctuates with energy levels and staffing changes.

Younger leaders may bring fresh ideas for outreach, but without mentorship and authority, those ideas rarely move beyond suggestion. Older leaders may carry deep conviction about evangelism, but without collaboration, those convictions struggle to translate into new forms of engagement.
The result is a church that values evangelism in theory but struggles to sustain it in practice.

Public Witness and Internal Inconsistency

The church's public witness is shaped not only by what it proclaims, but by how it lives internally. A congregation that preaches reconciliation but struggles to collaborate across generations sends mixed signals to the world.
In a polarized society, the church has a unique opportunity to model unity across difference. Generational diversity is one of the most visible forms of difference within congregations. When churches cannot navigate this diversity faithfully, their witness loses credibility.

Outsiders often observe how churches treat their own people before listening to what they say. A church that marginalizes younger voices or clings tightly to power structures may unintentionally communicate that faith is rigid rather than relational, exclusive rather than invitational.

Missional Sustainability and Leadership Succession

Mission is not only about reaching people today it is about sustaining faithfulness tomorrow. Churches that fail to prepare leaders across generations place their long-term mission at risk.
Leadership succession should be a missional priority, not an administrative afterthought. Without clear pathways for leadership development, churches become vulnerable during transitions. Momentum stalls. Vision fragments. Community trust weakens. Missional sustainability requires leaders who are formed, trusted, and empowered long before they are needed. This kind of preparation cannot happen in crisis; it must be cultivated over time.

A Theological Lens on Mission and Leadership

From a theological perspective, mission has always been generational. God's redemptive work unfolds through people who receive faith and pass it on. When churches disrupt this pattern, mission becomes disconnected from discipleship.
The generational leadership gap, therefore, undermines mission not by changing beliefs, but by weakening formation. Evangelism without discipleship becomes shallow. Discipleship without leadership development becomes stagnant. Leadership without generational continuity becomes fragile.
Mission thrives where leadership is shared, shaped, and sent across generations.

Section Summary

This section has argued that the generational leadership gap is not merely an internal leadership issue, but a missional concern with real consequences for evangelism, public witness, and long-term sustainability. Churches that fail to cultivate intergenerational leadership risk becoming disconnected from their communities and unprepared for the future.

In the next section, we will explore the biblical and theological roots of generational leadership, examining how Scripture frames leadership transfer, discipleship, and shared responsibility across time.

Section 4

A Biblical Vision of Leadership Across Generations

The generational leadership gap is not simply a modern organizational dilemma; it represents a departure from a deeply biblical pattern. Scripture consistently portrays leadership as something that is received, stewarded, and entrusted from one generation to the next. When churches struggle to share leadership across age groups, they are not only facing cultural pressure they are wrestling with theological obedience.

From the earliest pages of Scripture, faith is framed as a generational responsibility. God's covenantal work unfolds not in isolation, but through families, communities, and successive generations who remember, retell, and re-embody God's acts in history. Leadership, therefore, is never meant to terminate in one generation.

Remembering and Repeating: The Mandate of Psalm 78

Psalm 78 offers one of the clearest biblical mandates for generational continuity. The psalmist declares that the people of God are to tell "the coming generation the glorious deeds of the Lord, and his might, and the wonders that he has done." This instruction is not limited to storytelling; it encompasses formation, instruction, and leadership shaping.

The psalm goes on to explain why this transmission matters: so that future generations "should set their hope in God" and not forget His works. Memory and leadership are inseparable. When churches fail to pass on leadership, they risk passing on stories without stewardship.

This passage also reveals a critical truth: generational failure is not inevitable, but it is possible. Psalm 78 recounts moments where one generation failed to prepare the next, resulting in spiritual drift. The implication is sobering faith that is not intentionally transmitted weakens over time.

One Generation Declares to Another: Psalm 145 and Leadership Praise

Psalm 145:4 reinforces this vision: "One generation shall commend your works to another and shall declare your mighty acts." This declaration is more than verbal praise; it is embodied leadership. To commend God's works is to model trust, obedience, and responsibility.

In a leadership context, this means that older generations are called not merely to protect the church, but to actively prepare others to lead it. Likewise, younger generations are called not merely to receive instruction, but to step into responsibility shaped by wisdom.

When leadership is withheld, this biblical rhythm is disrupted. Praise remains, but proclamation loses embodiment. Testimony survives, but transfer does not.

Titus 2 and the Theology of Intentional Formation

The Apostle Paul's instruction in Titus 2 provides a practical theological framework for intergenerational formation. Older men and women are instructed to live in ways that model spiritual maturity, while younger believers are called to learn, grow, and assume responsibility.

This passage assumes relational proximity. Formation does not happen at a distance. Leadership development is not accidental; it is cultivated through example, instruction, and accountability.
Notably, Titus 2 does not frame generational interaction as optional or supplemental—it presents it as essential to the health of the faith community. When this model is neglected, leadership formation becomes fragmented, and discipleship becomes incomplete.

2 Timothy 2:2 and the Multiplication of Leadership

Perhaps the clearest leadership succession framework in Scripture appears in 2 Timothy 2:2: "What you have heard from me... entrust to faithful people who will be able to teach others also." This verse outlines a four-generation model of leadership transfer Paul to Timothy, Timothy to faithful people, faithful people to others.

This is not a theoretical model; it is a practical strategy for sustaining ministry. Leadership is multiplied, not hoarded. Authority is shared, not centralized. Faith is passed on, not preserved in isolation.

When churches fail to reflect this pattern, leadership becomes fragile. When they embrace it, leadership becomes resilient.

Leadership as Stewardship, Not Ownership

A key theological insight emerges from these texts: leadership in the church is a form of stewardship, not ownership. Leaders are caretakers of what God is doing in a particular season, not permanent gatekeepers of authority.

This understanding reshapes how leadership transitions are viewed. Stepping aside is not loss; it is faithfulness. Preparing others is not threat; it is obedience.

When churches adopt a stewardship mindset, leadership development becomes an act of worship rather than a concession to change.

Theological Consequences of Ignoring the Pattern

When churches neglect generational leadership formation, the consequences extend beyond organization. They affect theology itself. Faith becomes individualized rather than communal. Leadership becomes positional rather than relational. Ministry becomes reactive rather than reproductive.
Scripture presents a different vision one where leadership flows, multiplies, and adapts without losing integrity. This vision requires intentional effort, humility, and trust in God's work across time.

Section Summary

This section has demonstrated that generational leadership is not a modern innovation but a biblical mandate. Scripture consistently calls God's people to prepare, entrust, and empower future leaders. When churches ignore this pattern, they do not merely struggle organizationally, they drift theologically.

In the next section, we will explore how churches can begin reframing leadership as stewardship, moving from fear-based retention to faith-based release.

Section 5

From Ownership to Stewardship: Reframing How the Church Understands Leadership

One of the most significant barriers to bridging the generational leadership gap is not resistance to young leaders, but a deeply ingrained understanding of leadership itself. In many churches, leadership has been unconsciously framed as ownership rather than stewardship. Roles are held, guarded, and protected, often with good intentions, but without a clear theological framework for release.

This mindset is rarely articulated, yet it shapes culture powerfully. Leaders do not say, "This is my ministry," but their actions often communicate it. Decisions remain centralized. Authority is slow to transfer. Leadership roles remain fixed rather than fluid. Over time, stewardship gives way to possession.

Reframing leadership from ownership to stewardship is essential if churches are to cultivate intergenerational leadership without fear or fragmentation.

Leadership as a Sacred Trust

Biblically, leadership is never portrayed as a personal possession. It is a trust given for a season, accompanied by accountability and purpose. From Moses to Joshua, from Elijah to Elisha, from Paul to Timothy, leadership is transferred intentionally, relationally, and visibly.

These transitions were not accidental. They involved preparation, proximity, and public affirmation. The departing leader did not disappear, nor did the emerging leader ascend alone. Leadership moved forward through shared seasons, not abrupt handoffs.

When churches fail to plan for this kind of transition, leadership becomes static. When leaders see their role as something to be defended rather than stewarded, generational growth stalls.

Why Letting Go Feels So Difficult

Releasing leadership is rarely about ego alone. For many leaders, ministry roles are deeply tied to personal faith stories. They remember the seasons when no one else was willing to serve. They recall the sacrifices made to keep the church alive. Letting go can feel like erasing history.

Yet stewardship does not erase history, it extends it.
When leadership is stewarded well, legacy is preserved not through permanence, but through reproduction. The leader's influence multiplies rather than diminishes.

The difficulty arises when churches lack a theology of transition. Without language and models for healthy release, leaders default to what feels safe: staying in place.

The Cost of Holding Too Tightly

When leadership is held too tightly, unintended consequences emerge. Emerging leaders interpret caution as distrust. Innovation feels threatening. Leadership conversations become guarded rather than generative.

Over time, churches become dependent on a shrinking pool of leaders. Burnout increases. Younger leaders disengage not in rebellion, but in resignation. The church remains faithful, but fragile.

This fragility is not due to lack of commitment; it is due to lack of multiplication.

Stewardship Requires Shared Authority

Stewardship-oriented leadership requires more than delegation; it requires shared authority. Delegation assigns tasks while retaining control. Shared authority invites participation in discernment, decision-making, and responsibility.

This shift is uncomfortable because it introduces risk. Shared authority means mistakes will be made. Yet Scripture consistently shows that formation happens through responsibility, not observation.
Churches that refuse to share authority in the name of protection often undermine the very future they hope to secure.

Creating a Culture of Faith-Based Release

Faith-based release does not mean abandoning oversight. It means trusting God's work in others enough to walk with them as they grow. It involves mentoring rather than monitoring, coaching rather than controlling.

When leaders adopt a stewardship mindset, leadership development becomes intentional. Roles are viewed as training grounds. Transitions are anticipated rather than feared. Authority is seen as something to be shared for the sake of the mission.

This cultural shift does not happen overnight. It requires theological clarity, pastoral courage, and relational patience. But it is essential for generational continuity.

Section Summary

This section has reframed leadership as stewardship rather than ownership, highlighting why churches struggle to release authority and how that struggle impacts generational development. Without a theology of stewardship, leadership becomes static. With it, leadership becomes generative.
In the next section, we will conclude this chapter by naming the urgent call to action why churches must address the generational leadership gap now, not later.

Section 6

A Call to Courageous and Faithful Leadership

The generational leadership gap in the church is not the result of rebellion, irreverence, or generational failure. It is the consequence of good intentions left unstructured, faithfulness left unformed, and leadership left unexamined. Churches do not drift into generational division because they stop caring; they drift because they assume continuity will happen on its own.

This chapter has argued that the gap is real, persistent, and consequential. It manifests quietly in leadership meetings, ministry structures, and cultural assumptions. It persists even in healthy churches because fear goes unnamed, traditions go untranslated, and leadership pathways go unbuilt. Over time, what begins as caution becomes stagnation, and what was meant to preserve the church unintentionally limits its future.

At its core, the generational leadership gap is a theological problem before it is an organizational one. Scripture calls the people of God to remember, to entrust, and to prepare the next generation to lead faithfully. When churches fail to steward leadership across generations, they disrupt the biblical rhythm of discipleship and transmission. Leadership becomes positional rather than relational, static rather than generative.

This chapter has also shown that leadership gaps do not remain internal. They affect the church's mission, its public witness, and its capacity to engage a changing world. Churches that cannot model unity and collaboration across generations struggle to proclaim reconciliation with credibility. Mission weakens where leadership continuity is absent.

Yet the problem is not without hope. The same Scriptures that diagnose generational failure also provide a vision for generational faithfulness. Leadership, rightly understood, is stewardship. It is a sacred trust given for a season, meant to be shared, multiplied, and eventually released. When leaders adopt this posture, fear gives way to faith, and control gives way to collaboration.

The call before the church, then, is not to choose between honoring the past and embracing the future. It is to do both to honor faithfully by preparing intentionally. This requires courageous leadership willing to examine assumptions, challenge inherited structures, and create space for shared authority and formation.

Addressing the generational leadership gap cannot be postponed until a crisis forces change. By then, trust has eroded and preparation is incomplete. Faithful churches must act before leadership transitions become emergencies. They must move from assumption to intention, from preservation to participation, and from isolation to intergenerational partnership.

This chapter has named the problem clearly. The work ahead requires grounding that clarity in Scripture, theology, and disciplined practice. Only then can churches move from awareness to action.

Chapter 1 Summary

- The generational leadership gap is a present and pressing reality in many churches
- It persists due to fear, unclear structures, inherited systems, and unexamined assumptions
- Scripture presents leadership as generational, relational, and entrusted
- Leadership framed as ownership restricts growth; leadership framed as stewardship multiplies it
- The church's mission and witness are directly affected by how leadership is developed and shared

If the church is to respond faithfully to this challenge, it must begin where Scripture begins not with strategy, but with theology. Before structures can be built and pathways designed, leaders must recover a biblical vision of leadership that is generational by design and discipleship-driven at its core.

Chapter 2 will explore this vision in depth, examining how Scripture frames leadership formation, authority, and transfer across generations and why recovering this theology is essential for the future of the local church.

CHAPTER 2
A Biblical Theology of Generational Leadership

Section 1

Leadership Was Always Meant to Be Generational

Before leadership became a structure, a title, or an organizational function, it was a calling shaped by relationship and responsibility. Scripture presents leadership not as an isolated role reserved for a select few, but as a shared trust passed faithfully from one generation to the next. From Genesis to the early church, leadership develops through proximity, formation, and intentional transfer.

The Bible does not treat generational leadership as optional or circumstantial. It assumes that faith, authority, and responsibility will move forward through people who are prepared to receive them. When churches struggle to cultivate leadership across generations, they are not facing a new problem they are facing an old calling neglected.

God's Work Unfolds Across Generations

One of the most consistent themes in Scripture is that God's redemptive work unfolds over time, not in isolation. God introduces Himself repeatedly as "the God of Abraham, Isaac, and Jacob," emphasizing continuity rather than interruption. This self-identification is not merely historical; it is theological. It declares that God's purposes transcend individual lifetimes and require generational faithfulness.

Leadership, therefore, is not about preserving personal influence. It is about participating in a story larger than oneself. Each generation receives responsibility not to complete the work, but to advance it faithfully.

When leadership remains confined to one generation, the church inadvertently contradicts this biblical narrative. Faith becomes individualized, and leadership becomes episodic rather than cumulative.

Leadership as Formation, Not Position

Biblically, leadership emerges from formation long before it assumes function. Moses was formed in obscurity before leading publicly. David was shaped in the fields before sitting on the throne. Jesus formed His disciples relationally before sending them missionally.

This pattern reveals a crucial truth: leadership is not granted suddenly it is cultivated gradually. Generational leadership depends on shared life, not just shared space.

Churches that prioritize position over formation often struggle to develop leaders across generations. Without intentional discipleship and mentoring, leadership becomes something one waits for rather than grows into.

The Cost of Skipping Generational Formation

When churches neglect generational formation, leadership gaps widen. Emerging leaders lack confidence and clarity. Senior leaders feel pressure to remain in place. Succession becomes reactive rather than intentional.

Scripture warns against this pattern implicitly. Faith that is not taught, modeled, and entrusted weakens over time. Leadership that is not formed relationally becomes fragile.

The biblical vision of leadership does not support independence; it depends on inheritance and entrustment.

Faith Received and Faith Entrusted

The New Testament reinforces this generational framework. Paul's letters consistently emphasize transmission. Faith is received, guarded, and passed on. Leadership emerges through mentoring relationships and shared ministry.

Paul does not instruct Timothy to lead alone. He instructs him to entrust leadership to others who will, in turn, teach still others. This chain of transmission reveals that leadership sustainability is a theological responsibility, not merely an organizational concern.

Churches that embrace this vision view leadership development as a sacred task. Churches that ignore it often struggle with continuity, unity, and long-term impact.

Section Summary

This section has established that leadership in Scripture is inherently generational. God's work unfolds through successive generations who receive, steward, and entrust leadership faithfully. When churches neglect this pattern, leadership becomes isolated and fragile. When they recover it, leadership becomes resilient and reproductive.

In the next section, we will explore how Scripture frames authority and responsibility across generations, addressing common misconceptions that hinder shared leadership in the church.

Section 2

Authority, Responsibility, and the Shared Nature of Leadership

One of the greatest obstacles to intergenerational leadership in the church is a misunderstanding of authority. Many leadership tensions across generations are not rooted in unwillingness to serve, but in confusion about who holds authority, how it is exercised, and when it is entrusted to others. Scripture offers a clear and compelling vision of authority one that is shared, stewarded, and always accountable to God.

Biblical authority is never self-generated. It is given, affirmed, and exercised in community. When churches treat authority as something to be protected rather than something to be entrusted, generational leadership stalls.

Authority Comes From God, Not Position

Throughout Scripture, authority originates with God, not with age, tenure, or title. Leaders are appointed, affirmed, and empowered by God for the sake of the community. This theological truth reorients how leadership should function within the church.

Moses did not claim authority; he received it. Joshua did not seize leadership; it was publicly affirmed. The disciples did not appoint themselves; they were called and sent. Authority in Scripture is always derived, never owned.

This distinction matters greatly in generational contexts. When authority is viewed as possession, leaders guard it. When authority is viewed as stewardship, leaders share it.

Shared Authority in the Old Testament

The Old Testament provides multiple examples of shared leadership. Moses led Israel, yet leadership was distributed among elders, judges, and tribal leaders. When Moses attempted to lead alone, he was corrected and instructed to share responsibility.

This distribution of leadership was not a sign of weakness; it was a sign of wisdom. Shared authority allowed leadership to be sustainable and accessible across generations. It also created space for emerging leaders to grow under guidance rather than pressure.

Importantly, shared leadership did not diminish Moses' role it strengthened the community.

Jesus and the Reframing of Authority

Jesus radically reframed authority in the New Testament. He consistently challenged hierarchical assumptions, teaching His disciples that leadership in the Kingdom of God looks different from leadership in the world. Authority was not to be exercised through dominance, but through service.

Jesus did not withhold authority from His disciples until they were perfect. He entrusted them with responsibility while they were still learning. He sent them out, allowed them to struggle, corrected them, and sent them again.

This pattern reveals a critical truth: authority is formative. People grow into leadership by exercising responsibility under guidance, not by waiting indefinitely for readiness.

Responsibility as a Pathway to Formation

Biblical leadership formation involves responsibility. Scripture does not support the idea that leaders must be fully prepared before being entrusted with authority. Instead, it shows that formation often happens through responsibility itself.
When churches withhold responsibility in the name of protection, they inadvertently hinder formation. Younger leaders remain untested. Older leaders remain overextended. The community loses the benefit of shared discernment.

Responsibility, when paired with mentoring and accountability, becomes a powerful tool for growth across generations.

Power, Control, and Trust

At the heart of many generational leadership conflicts lies the issue of trust. Authority requires trust trust in God's work in others, trust in the formation process, and trust that mistakes can become moments of growth rather than failure.
Scripture does not deny the risk involved in sharing authority. It acknowledges it. Yet it consistently affirms that trust, not control, is the posture of faithful leadership.

Churches that emphasize control over trust may preserve order, but they limit growth. Churches that cultivate trust alongside accountability create environments where leadership can flourish across generations.

Authority That Builds, Not Blocks

Paul's letters frequently describe authority as something given "for building up, not tearing down." Authority is meant to strengthen the body, not restrict it. When authority is exercised to protect position rather than empower people, it contradicts its biblical purpose.

Intergenerational leadership thrives when authority is used to create access, opportunity, and growth not to reinforce distance or hierarchy.

Section Summary

This section has reframed authority as a shared, stewarded gift rather than a guarded possession. Scripture presents authority as something given by God, exercised in community, and entrusted across generations for the sake of formation and mission. When churches misunderstand authority, leadership gaps widen. When they recover its biblical purpose, leadership becomes collaborative and generative.

In the next section, we will examine how Scripture frames mentorship, discipleship, and relational proximity as essential to generational leadership development.

Section 3

Mentorship, Discipleship, and the Power of Proximity

Scripture does not present leadership development as a curriculum to be completed, but as a **relationship to be lived**. From the earliest biblical narratives to the formation of the early church, leadership emerges through proximity shared life, shared struggle, and shared obedience. Mentorship and discipleship are not optional supplements to leadership development; they are the means by which leadership is formed.

When churches attempt to cultivate leaders without relational proximity, they often produce competence without character and confidence without maturity. The biblical model offers a different path one where leadership grows through presence, modeling, and trust over time.

The Elijah and Elisha Model of Relational Formation

One of the clearest examples of generational leadership formation appears in the relationship between Elijah and Elisha. Elisha does not receive leadership through a formal appointment alone; he receives it through sustained proximity. He walks with Elijah, observes his ministry, participates in moments of challenge, and remains faithful even when tested.

The transfer of leadership is public, relational, and spiritual. Elijah does not disappear before Elisha is ready, nor does Elisha step into leadership without preparation. The relationship allows wisdom, authority, and responsibility to pass organically.

This narrative illustrates a key principle: leadership is transferred through relationship before it is transferred through role.

Jesus and the Formation of the Twelve

Jesus' approach to leadership formation reinforces this principle. He did not gather His disciples for occasional instruction; He invited them into daily life. They traveled together, ate together, served together, and struggled together. Through proximity, Jesus shaped their understanding of authority, mission, and faith.

Notably, Jesus entrusted His disciples with responsibility long before they fully understood His mission. He allowed them to preach, heal, and lead even as they made mistakes. Formation happened through engagement, correction, and continued relationship.

This model challenges churches that delay leadership development until individuals appear fully prepared. Scripture suggests that preparation often occurs through responsibility, not prior to it.

Paul and Timothy: Mentorship Across Generations

The relationship between Paul and Timothy provides a New Testament model of intergenerational mentorship. Paul refers to Timothy not merely as a coworker, but as a son in the faith. Their relationship is marked by instruction, encouragement, correction, and trust.

Paul does not isolate Timothy from leadership challenges; he involves him. He sends Timothy into difficult contexts, equips him through letters, and affirms his authority publicly. This mentorship is both personal and missional.

The result is leadership continuity rooted in relationship rather than position.

Discipleship That Leads to Leadership

Biblical discipleship is inherently directional it moves people toward responsibility. When discipleship is disconnected from leadership development, churches may produce spiritually mature individuals who are uncertain how to serve beyond personal faith.

Scripture does not separate discipleship from leadership formation. Those who are discipled are expected to disciple others. Those who are taught are expected to teach. This progression requires intentional mentoring relationships that guide emerging leaders into deeper responsibility.

The Cost of Distance

When relational proximity is absent, leadership development becomes transactional. Training replaces mentoring. Observation replaces participation. Feedback becomes infrequent or impersonal.

Distance limits trust. Without trust, authority is withheld. Without authority, leadership stalls. This cycle reinforces generational gaps and weakens continuity.

Churches that prioritize proximity create environments where leadership grows naturally. Churches that prioritize efficiency over relationship often struggle to develop leaders across generations.

Creating Cultures of Relational Formation

Cultivating relational mentorship requires intentionality. It means structuring ministry in ways that encourage shared leadership, shared experiences, and shared discernment. It means valuing presence as much as productivity.

Relational formation cannot be rushed, but it can be nurtured. When churches create space for mentoring relationships to flourish, they align themselves with Scripture's vision of generational leadership.

Section Summary

This section has shown that mentorship and discipleship are the biblical foundations of generational leadership. Leadership is formed through proximity, responsibility, and relationship not merely through instruction or tenure. When churches recover this model, leadership development becomes natural and sustainable. When they neglect it, leadership becomes fragmented and fragile.

In the next section, we will explore how Scripture frames the role of community in leadership formation, examining the church as a collective environment where generational leadership is shaped.

Section 4

Leadership Formed in Community, Not in Isolation

Scripture consistently presents leadership as something that emerges within community rather than apart from it. While individual calling and gifting are affirmed, leadership formation is never portrayed as a solitary journey. Instead, the people of God function as a body a living organism in which growth, discernment, and responsibility are shared.

This communal vision of leadership has significant implications for how churches approach generational development. Leadership is not produced through isolation or competition, but through belonging, accountability, and shared life.

The Body of Christ as a Formative Environment

The Apostle Paul's imagery of the church as the body of Christ emphasizes interdependence rather than hierarchy. Each part has a role, and each role contributes to the health of the whole. No single generation embodies the fullness of the church's calling.

In this framework, leadership formation is not reserved for elite spaces. It unfolds within worship, service, conflict, reconciliation, and mission. Community becomes the context in which leaders learn humility, cooperation, and discernment.
When churches fragment leadership by age or isolate generations into silos, they undermine this biblical vision. The body cannot function fully when its parts are disconnected.

Shared Discernment Across Generations

Biblical leadership is communal not only in practice, but in discernment. Throughout Scripture, important decisions are made through collective prayer, conversation, and reflection. The early church models this clearly, engaging leaders and congregations together in discernment.

Generational diversity enriches this process. Older leaders contribute wisdom shaped by experience and memory. Younger leaders contribute insight shaped by context and innovation. When these perspectives are integrated, discernment becomes more faithful and comprehensive.

Churches that limit discernment to a single generation risk blind spots. Churches that embrace intergenerational discernment strengthen their capacity to respond wisely to God's leading.

Community as a School of Leadership

The church functions as a school not in the formal sense, but in the formative sense. Leaders learn by participating in the life of the community. They observe conflict resolution, pastoral care, mission engagement, and worship leadership firsthand.
This communal formation requires transparency. Mistakes must be treated as learning opportunities rather than failures. Authority must be exercised in ways that invite growth rather than suppress participation.

When communities create safe spaces for learning and growth, leadership flourishes across generations.

Accountability and Mutual Submission

Scripture calls believers to submit to one another out of reverence for Christ. This mutual submission shapes how leadership is exercised and received. Authority is balanced by accountability, and leadership is shaped by relationship.

In generational contexts, mutual submission challenges both older and younger leaders. Older leaders are called to listen and release control. Younger leaders are called to receive guidance and honor experience. Both are called to humility.

This posture creates a culture where leadership is not competitive, but collaborative.

Community That Sends, Not Stagnates

Biblical communities do not exist solely for internal growth; they exist to be sent. Leadership formation within community prepares individuals for mission beyond the community.

When churches embrace communal leadership formation, they cultivate leaders who are rooted, resilient, and ready to serve beyond themselves. Generational continuity ensures that mission extends beyond any single leader or era.

Section Summary

This section has emphasized that leadership formation in Scripture occurs within community. The body of Christ functions as the environment in which leaders are shaped, discernment is shared, and authority is balanced by accountability. When churches recover this communal vision, generational leadership becomes possible and sustainable.

In the next section, we will examine the role of the Holy Spirit in generational leadership, exploring how spiritual empowerment transcends age and experience.

Section 5

The Role of the Holy Spirit in Generational Leadership

Any discussion of leadership in the church that neglects the work of the Holy Spirit remains incomplete. Scripture makes clear that leadership formation, authority, and continuity are ultimately Spirit-empowered realities. While structures, mentorship, and community provide necessary frameworks, it is the Spirit of God who animates, equips, and sustains leadership across generations.

The generational leadership gap cannot be bridged through strategy alone. It requires spiritual discernment, obedience, and dependence on the Spirit's work within and among God's people.

The Spirit Transcends Age and Experience

One of the defining characteristics of the Holy Spirit's work is that it transcends human categories, including age, status, and experience. The prophet Joel proclaimed that God would pour out His Spirit on "all flesh," resulting in sons and daughters prophesying, young men seeing visions, and old men dreaming dreams. This promise, later affirmed in Acts, establishes a foundational truth: spiritual empowerment is not limited by generation.
This vision challenges leadership cultures that privilege age alone or novelty alone. The Spirit empowers both youth and elders, not in competition, but in collaboration. When churches resist sharing leadership across generations, they often resist the Spirit's inclusive work, sometimes unknowingly.

Pentecost and the Birth of a Multigenerational Church

The event of Pentecost marks the birth of the church as a Spirit-formed, generationally diverse community. The Spirit does not descend upon a homogenous group, but upon a gathered community representing various ages, backgrounds, and experiences.

From the outset, leadership in the church emerges through the Spirit's gifting rather than human qualification alone. Authority is affirmed through spiritual fruit, obedience, and communal recognition.

Pentecost reminds the church that leadership continuity depends not only on human preparation, but on openness to the Spirit's ongoing work.

Spiritual Discernment and Leadership Transfer

In Scripture, leadership transitions are often accompanied by prayer, fasting, and discernment. The Spirit guides the community in recognizing whom God is calling and how authority should be entrusted.
This spiritual discernment is particularly important in generational leadership contexts. Without prayerful discernment, leadership decisions default to comfort, habit, or fear. With discernment, churches are able to release control and trust the Spirit's guidance.

Leadership transfer, therefore, becomes an act of faith rather than anxiety.

The Spirit as Teacher and Guide

Jesus promised that the Holy Spirit would guide His followers into truth. This promise applies not only to personal faith, but to communal leadership formation. The Spirit teaches, convicts, corrects, and encourages leaders across generations.
This ongoing guidance allows churches to adapt without losing theological integrity. The Spirit does not contradict Scripture but illuminates it in new contexts. Generational leadership thrives where churches remain attentive to this guiding presence.

Power for Witness and Continuity

The Spirit empowers leadership not for status, but for witness. Leadership that flows from the Spirit remains oriented toward mission rather than preservation. It seeks to build the body and extend the gospel.

When churches rely solely on human strength to sustain leadership, fatigue and fear increase. When they rely on the Spirit, renewal becomes possible. The Spirit enables leaders to release control, trust others, and embrace generational collaboration.

Section Summary

This section has highlighted the essential role of the Holy Spirit in generational leadership. Scripture affirms that leadership is Spirit-empowered, transcending age and experience. The Spirit forms, guides, and sustains leadership continuity, enabling the church to move forward with faith rather than fear.

In the final section of this chapter, we will draw these theological themes together and articulate a cohesive biblical framework for generational leadership, preparing the reader for practical application in subsequent chapters.

Section 6

Recovering a Faithful and Generational Vision of Leadership

This chapter has argued that generational leadership is not a contemporary innovation, but a biblical expectation woven throughout Scripture. From the covenantal identity of God as the God of successive generations to the Spirit-empowered formation of the early church, leadership in God's economy is always received, stewarded, and entrusted.

Scripture presents leadership as a sacred trust rather than a personal possession. Authority is derived from God, exercised in community, and shared for the sake of formation and mission. Mentorship and discipleship function as the relational engines of leadership development, while the community of faith provides the environment in which leaders are shaped and discerned. Above all, the Holy Spirit empowers leadership across generations, transcending human limitations and sustaining continuity.

When churches neglect this theological vision, leadership becomes isolated, fragile, and fear driven. Faith may be preserved, but it is not always passed on. Authority may be exercised, but it is not always entrusted. Mission may continue, but it lacks sustainability.
This chapter has also revealed that many of the church's leadership challenges stem not from lack of commitment, but from theological drift. When leadership is framed primarily as position rather than stewardship, or as control rather than trust, churches depart often unintentionally from Scripture's generational design.

Recovering a biblical theology of generational leadership requires humility and courage. It calls leaders to examine inherited assumptions, relinquish fear-based practices, and realign leadership culture with God's redemptive rhythm. It challenges churches to view leadership development as an act of obedience rather than a concession to change.

This theological recovery does not diminish tradition it fulfills it. When leadership is stewarded faithfully across generations, the church honors its past by preparing its future. Memory becomes mission, and heritage becomes hope.

Chapter 2 Summary

- Leadership in Scripture is inherently generational
- Authority is derived from God and meant to be shared and entrusted
- Mentorship and discipleship are central to leadership formation
- Community provides the context for growth and accountability
- The Holy Spirit empowers leadership across generations
- Generational leadership is a theological mandate, not a strategic option

Theological clarity alone, however, does not guarantee faithful practice. Even churches that affirm a biblical vision of generational leadership often struggle to live it out. Fear, control, conflict, and unresolved power dynamics can distort theology and hinder implementation.

Chapter 3 will examine why churches resist change even when theology is clear, exploring the emotional, cultural, and organizational barriers that prevent generational leadership from taking root. This chapter will move from biblical vision to honest diagnosis naming the obstacles that must be addressed before solutions can succeed.

CHAPTER 3
Why Churches Struggle to Change What They Can Clearly See

Section 1

When Theology Is Clear, but Practice Is Complicated

Most churches do not struggle with generational leadership because they lack biblical knowledge. Many pastors and leaders can readily affirm that leadership should be developed, shared, and entrusted across generations. They preach it. They teach it. They may even agree with it in principle. Yet agreement does not always translate into action.

This disconnect between theological clarity and practical implementation is one of the most persistent challenges facing the church today. Leaders may see the problem clearly yet feel unable or unwilling to address it meaningfully. The result is frustration, delay, and eventually stagnation.

Understanding this resistance requires looking beyond doctrine and into the human realities that shape church life.

The Gap Between Belief and Behavior

Churches are not merely theological institutions; they are relational communities shaped by history, emotion, and shared experience. Even when leaders affirm a biblical vision of generational leadership, deeply embedded patterns can override conviction.

Belief answers the question what should be.
Behavior reveals what feels safe.

In many congregations, leadership practices are guided less by theology and more by memory, fear, and habit. What has "worked before" becomes the default measure of faithfulness. Change, even, when necessary, feels risky.

This is why churches can preach faith while practicing caution, affirm trust while maintaining control, and celebrate growth while resisting transition.

Emotional Attachments to Roles and Identity

One of the most significant barriers to change is emotional attachment. Leadership roles are rarely neutral. They carry meaning, affirmation, and identity. For many long-serving leaders, ministry roles are tied to personal sacrifice, spiritual growth, and seasons of hardship endured for the sake of the church.

Letting go of leadership, therefore, can feel like letting go of purpose. This attachment is rarely expressed openly. Leaders do not say, "I am afraid to step aside." Instead, resistance appears in more subtle forms:
- "Now is not the right time."
- "We don't have anyone ready."
- "We need to protect the church."
- "We've always done it this way."

These statements are not necessarily dishonest, they are protective. They reveal an underlying fear that change may erase legacy or destabilize identity.

Fear of What Comes After Release

Change introduces uncertainty. Releasing leadership raises questions that feel threatening:
- What if the next generation fails?
- What if traditions are altered?
- What if the church loses stability?

- What if my voice no longer matters?

Fear of the unknown often outweighs confidence in God's ongoing work. As a result, churches delay transition, hoping clarity will emerge without risk.

Yet Scripture consistently shows that leadership transition requires faith, not certainty. Waiting for perfect readiness often becomes a way of avoiding obedience.

Organizational Comfort and Inherited Patterns

Beyond emotional resistance, churches are shaped by organizational inertia. Leadership structures, bylaws, committees, and traditions often reflect the needs of a previous era. These systems may still function, but they are rarely evaluated critically.

Because these patterns are familiar, they feel trustworthy. Because they are inherited, they feel unquestionable.
Organizational comfort discourages experimentation. Emerging leaders are expected to adapt to existing systems rather than being invited to help reimagine them. Innovation becomes threatening because it exposes the limits of current structures.

The Illusion of Stability

One of the most deceptive forms of resistance is the illusion of stability. Churches may appear stable on the surface services continue, finances are managed, programs operate—but beneath that stability lies fragility.

Leadership pipelines remain thin. Decision-making depends on a few individuals. Ministry momentum slows quietly.
Stability without succession is temporary.

When churches mistake stillness for health, they postpone the work of leadership development until crisis forces change. At that point, trust is low and preparation is incomplete.

Section Summary

This section has identified why churches struggle to act even when theology is clear. Emotional attachment, fear of loss, organizational comfort, and the illusion of stability combine to resist change. These forces do not reflect a lack of faith, but a lack of intentional reflection and courageous leadership.

In the next section, we will examine how power, control, and unspoken hierarchies shape leadership culture and why addressing these dynamics is essential for generational growth.

Section 2

Power, Control, and the Unspoken Hierarchies of Church Leadership

While fear and emotional attachment explain part of the resistance to generational leadership, they do not tell the whole story. Beneath many leadership tensions lies a deeper dynamic: power. Power in churches is rarely discussed openly, yet it quietly shapes who is heard, who decides, and who is trusted.

Unlike formal authority, power often operates informally. It is embedded in relationships, history, reputation, and influence. Over time, these dynamics solidify into unspoken hierarchies that shape leadership culture often without conscious intent.

Understanding these hierarchies is essential if churches are to move from generational stagnation to generational collaboration.

Informal Power Versus Formal Authority

In many congregations, formal authority is defined by titles, offices, and organizational charts. Informal power, however, operates beneath the surface. It belongs to those who have:
- Long-standing relationships
- Institutional memory
- Financial influence
- Cultural credibility
- Historical significance

This power is not inherently harmful. In fact, it often reflects deep commitment and faithfulness. Problems arise when informal power is exercised without accountability or when it becomes resistant to shared leadership.

Emerging leaders quickly learn where real power resides not by reading bylaws, but by observing whose voices shape decisions. When power remains concentrated within one generation, leadership development across generations becomes difficult, regardless of formal structures.

Control as a Response to Uncertainty

Control often emerges as a response to uncertainty rather than a desire for dominance. When leaders feel responsible for protecting the church, they may tighten control to prevent perceived threats.

This control can manifest in subtle ways:
- Limiting decision-making input
- Requiring excessive approval processes
- Discouraging experimentation
- Framing innovation as risk rather than opportunity

While control may preserve order in the short term, it undermines trust in the long term. Emerging leaders interpret control as lack of confidence. Over time, initiative diminishes and engagement declines.

The Theology of Control Versus the Theology of Trust

Scripture offers a clear contrast between control and trust. God repeatedly calls leaders to trust His ongoing work in others rather than relying solely on personal oversight. Authority is exercised through service, humility, and faith not domination.
When churches operate from a theology of control, leadership becomes guarded and hierarchical. When they operate from a theology of trust, leadership becomes relational and generative.
Trust does not eliminate accountability. It reframes it. Leaders remain responsible, but they share responsibility rather than hoarding it.

Unspoken Rules and Cultural Barriers

Many leadership barriers are enforced not by policy, but by culture. Unspoken rules shape behavior:
- "We don't question senior leaders."
- "Young people need to wait their turn."
- "This is how we've always done it."

These rules are rarely written down, yet they are deeply influential. They create invisible boundaries that emerging leaders must navigate without guidance.

When churches fail to name and examine these cultural norms, they remain unchallenged. Leadership development becomes constrained by tradition rather than guided by theology.

Power, Age, and Spiritual Authority

In some contexts, age is equated with spiritual authority. While experience and wisdom deserve honor, Scripture does not equate maturity with age alone. Spiritual authority flows from character, calling, and fruit not chronology.

When age becomes the primary marker of authority, younger leaders struggle to be seen as legitimate. This dynamic not only discourages leadership development but also contradicts Scripture's emphasis on gifting and calling.

The Cost of Avoiding Power Conversations

Churches often avoid conversations about power because they fear conflict. Yet avoiding these conversations allows unhealthy dynamics to persist. Silence protects the status quo and perpetuates inequality.

Healthy churches do not eliminate power; they redeem it. They acknowledge influence, distribute authority, and create transparent processes that invite participation across generations.

Section Summary

This section has examined how power, control, and unspoken hierarchies shape leadership culture in ways that hinder generational collaboration. Informal power, fear-based control, and unexamined traditions often restrict leadership development, even in well-intentioned churches.

In the next section, we will explore how conflict avoidance and fear of division prevent churches from addressing these dynamics and why courageous conversation is essential for change.

Section 3

When the Fear of Division Becomes a Barrier to Faithful Change

Few values are cherished more deeply in the church than unity. Scripture calls believers to live in harmony, to pursue peace, and to guard the bond of fellowship. Because of this, many churches go to great lengths to avoid conflict, often believing that avoiding tension is synonymous with preserving unity.
Yet one of the great paradoxes of church leadership is this: the very desire to protect unity can become a barrier to faithful change.

In congregations where unity is emphasized without clarity, difficult conversations are postponed, tensions are spiritualized, and leadership challenges remain unresolved. Over time, the fear of division becomes more influential than the call to growth.

Conflict Avoidance as a Leadership Strategy

Conflict avoidance often masquerades as spiritual maturity. Leaders pride themselves on being "peacemakers," avoiding controversy, and keeping everyone comfortable. While peacemaking is biblical, avoiding necessary conflict is not the same as pursuing peace.
Peace in Scripture is not the absence of tension; it is the presence of justice, truth, and reconciliation.

When leaders avoid conversations about generational leadership because they fear upsetting long-standing members or alienating emerging leaders, they unintentionally allow underlying issues to deepen. Silence becomes strategy. Delay becomes discipline. Nothing changes and the cost accumulates.

Unity Anxiety and Leadership Paralysis

Many churches suffer from what can be called unity anxiety a constant fear that addressing difficult issues will fracture the congregation. This anxiety is especially pronounced in churches with a strong sense of history or in communities that have survived previous conflict.

Leaders may think:
- "We've already been through enough."
- "We don't want to reopen old wounds."
- "This could divide the church."

As a result, necessary leadership conversations are framed as threats rather than opportunities. The church chooses short-term calm over long-term health.

Ironically, unresolved tension often causes more damage than honest dialogue. What is avoided publicly is discussed privately. Frustration spreads quietly. Trust erodes slowly.

Unity Without Truth Is Fragile

Scripture consistently links unity with truth. Unity built on silence is unstable. Unity sustained by avoidance cannot endure seasons of transition or change.

Biblical unity does not require uniformity of opinion, but it does require shared commitment to truth and growth. Leaders are called to shepherd people through tension, not around it.
Generational leadership development inevitably raises questions about authority, tradition, and change. Avoiding these questions does not preserve unity, it postpones conflict until it becomes unmanageable.

The Cost to Emerging Leaders

Conflict avoidance disproportionately affects emerging leaders. When difficult conversations are suppressed, younger leaders often interpret silence as dismissal. They may assume their concerns are unwelcome or their presence is merely symbolic.

Over time, they disengage not out of rebellion, but out of resignation. The church loses potential leaders not because they were rejected explicitly, but because they were never invited into honest conversation.

This quiet disengagement is one of the most damaging consequences of unity anxiety.

Courageous Conversation as Pastoral Care

Addressing generational leadership challenges requires courageous conversation. This does not mean confrontation for its own sake, nor does it mean disregarding relationships. It means naming reality with humility, patience, and faith.
Pastoral leadership involves guiding people through discomfort toward deeper understanding. Courageous conversations create space for mutual listening, repentance, and growth.
When churches frame these conversations as acts of care rather than threats to unity, transformation becomes possible.

Peace That Produces Growth

Scripture envisions peace as something that produces righteousness and growth. True peace allows the church to confront difficult truths without fear, trusting that God is at work in the process.

Generational leadership thrives where churches prioritize peace with purpose, peace that embraces honesty, fosters trust, and prepares the body for future faithfulness.

Section Summary

This section has shown that fear of division and conflict avoidance often prevent churches from addressing generational leadership challenges. Unity without truth is fragile, and peace without courage is incomplete. Churches that avoid difficult conversations risk losing emerging leaders and weakening long-term health.

In the next section, we will explore how unresolved conflict and avoidance shape church culture over time, creating patterns that resist change and reinforce generational divides.

Section 4

When Avoidance Becomes Culture and Culture Resists Change

Church culture does not form overnight. It is shaped gradually by repeated decisions, unspoken expectations, and unresolved tensions. What begins as a temporary response to conflict or uncertainty can, over time, become a defining feature of how a church operates. When generational leadership challenges go unaddressed, avoidance slowly hardens into culture.

This is one of the most difficult realities for churches to confront, because culture often feels invisible to those living within it. What outsiders may recognize immediately, insiders may interpret as normal, faithful, or even spiritual.

How Patterns Become Norms

Every church develops patterns ways of making decisions, handling disagreement, and distributing responsibility. When leadership avoids difficult conversations or delays necessary transitions, those choices communicate values, even if unintentionally.

Over time, these patterns become norms:
- Leadership roles remain static
- Decision-making stays centralized
- New ideas are quietly filtered out
- Younger voices learn when to speak and when not to

Eventually, these norms are no longer questioned. They become "the way things are done," and any attempt to challenge them is perceived as disruptive rather than discerning.

Cultural Memory and Institutional Inertia

Churches carry long memories. Past conflicts, painful transitions, or near-splits shape how future decisions are approached. While remembering the past can protect a church from repeating mistakes, it can also trap the church in fear.
Institutional inertia sets in when past pain dictates present practice. Leaders become cautious not because the current situation demands it, but because history warns them against risk.

As a result, leadership development becomes reactive rather than proactive. Churches wait until change is unavoidable instead of preparing for it intentionally.

When Stability Masks Fragility

Cultural avoidance often presents itself as stability. Services run smoothly. Ministries function consistently. Conflict appears minimal. Yet beneath this stability lies fragility.

Leadership pipelines are thin. Succession plans are unclear. Authority rests on individuals rather than systems. When unexpected change occurs, the church struggles to adapt.
Stability without renewal creates the illusion of health while weakening resilience.

The Silencing Effect of Culture

One of the most damaging effects of avoidance-based culture is silence. Emerging leaders learn which topics are off-limits. Questions about leadership transition, authority, or innovation are discouraged not explicitly, but relationally.

Silence becomes a survival skill. Those who speak up risk being labeled divisive or impatient. Those who remain quiet are rewarded with acceptance.

Over time, the church loses not only voices, but vision.

Culture Shapes What Feels Faithful

Perhaps the most troubling aspect of cultural avoidance is that it reshapes how faithfulness is defined. Obedience becomes equated with compliance. Loyalty becomes equated with silence. Unity becomes equated with sameness.
These definitions are rarely intentional, but they are powerful. They shape how Scripture is interpreted, how leadership is exercised, and how change is evaluated.

Culture, once formed, begins to defend itself. Any attempt to introduce generational leadership development feels foreign even threatening because it challenges deeply embedded assumptions.

Naming Culture Is the First Step Toward Change

Churches cannot change what they are unwilling to name. Cultural patterns must be brought into the light before they can be reshaped. This requires humility, courage, and pastoral sensitivity.
Naming culture does not mean assigning blame. It means recognizing reality. It means acknowledging how past decisions continue to shape present practice.

When leaders name culture honestly, they create space for repentance, renewal, and redirection.

Section Summary

This section has shown how avoidance, left unchecked, becomes culture and how culture resists change. What begins as caution hardens into custom, silencing emerging leaders and weakening leadership continuity. Stability masks fragility, and faithfulness is redefined by comfort rather than calling.

In the final section of this chapter, we will issue a clear call to courageous leadership, emphasizing why confronting these realities is necessary for generational renewal and long-term faithfulness.

Section 5

The Courage to Name What Is Holding the Church Back

The struggle to change what is clearly seen is not primarily a problem of awareness, it is a problem of courage. Churches often recognize generational leadership challenges long before they address them. Leaders feel the tension, observe the patterns, and sense the growing disconnect. What delays change is not ignorance, but hesitation.

This chapter has shown that resistance to generational leadership development is rarely malicious. It is shaped by fear, emotional attachment, power dynamics, conflict avoidance, and cultural inertia. These forces do not operate independently; they reinforce one another, creating environments where maintaining the status quo feels safer than stepping into faith-filled change.

Yet safety and faithfulness are not the same.

Leadership Responsibility and Spiritual Stewardship

Scripture consistently holds leaders responsible not only for what they preserve, but for what they prepare. Shepherds are called to guide the flock forward, not merely keep it intact. When leaders avoid necessary change in the name of peace, they may unintentionally compromise long-term health.

Leadership responsibility includes the willingness to confront uncomfortable realities, to name cultural patterns honestly, and to invite the community into growth. Avoiding this responsibility does not protect the church, it postpones formation and weakens resilience.

Faithful leadership requires more than good intentions; it requires intentional action.

Courage Is a Spiritual Discipline

Courage in church leadership is not rooted in personality or confidence; it is rooted in trust in God. Leaders are called to act not because outcomes are guaranteed, but because obedience is required.

Naming generational leadership gaps, power imbalances, and cultural avoidance is an act of spiritual discipline. It reflects confidence that God is present in the process and capable of sustaining the church through change.

Courage allows leaders to move beyond fear-based preservation into faith-based stewardship.

From Diagnosis to Direction

This chapter has focused on diagnosis naming why churches struggle to change what they can clearly see. Diagnosis, however, is not the end goal. It is the necessary foundation for direction.

Without honest diagnosis, solutions remain superficial. Programs fail. Initiatives stall. Frustration grows. But when leaders confront reality truthfully, they create the conditions for transformation.

The purpose of this chapter is not to discourage, but to clarify. Change becomes possible when leaders understand what has been holding them back.

Hope Beyond Resistance

Despite the depth of the challenges outlined in this chapter, there is reason for hope. Churches are not trapped by their past. Cultures can be reshaped. Leadership practices can be reimagined. Generational collaboration can be cultivated.

Hope does not deny resistance it overcomes it through intentional faithfulness. When leaders acknowledge fear, address power dynamics, and engage courageous conversation, they open pathways for renewal.

Chapter 3 Summary
- Churches often struggle to change despite theological clarity
- Emotional attachment, fear, and organizational comfort resist transition
- Power and unspoken hierarchies shape leadership culture
- Conflict avoidance undermines unity and growth
- Avoidance hardens into culture over time
- Courageous leadership is required to move forward

With the barriers now named, the path forward becomes clearer. Theology provides the vision. Diagnosis reveals the obstacles. The next step is intentional construction building leadership pathways that make generational collaboration possible.

Chapter 4 will move from problem to practice, outlining how churches can develop intergenerational leadership pipelines that are biblically grounded, relationally wise, and practically sustainable.

CHAPTER 4
From Calling to Capacity: Building Intergenerational Leadership Pipelines

Section 1

Why Churches Need Pipelines, Not Just Passion

Most churches do not lack passionate people. They lack pathways. Across generations, individuals express a desire to serve, to grow, and to contribute meaningfully to the life of the church. Young adults want to be involved. Middle-aged leaders want to be effective. Senior leaders want the church to thrive beyond their tenure. Yet without intentional leadership pipelines, passion often goes unused, misdirected, or eventually lost.

A leadership pipeline is not a corporate concept imposed on the church. It is a biblical necessity that ensures calling is matched with capacity and opportunity. Without pipelines, leadership development remains accidental rather than intentional.

Calling Without Capacity Creates Frustration

In many churches, calling is affirmed verbally but unsupported structurally. Leaders tell emerging members, "You are gifted," "God has a calling on your life," or "We see leadership in you." While affirming, these statements often lack follow-through.
Without clear pathways, affirmation becomes ambiguous. Emerging leaders are left asking:
- What comes next?
- How do I grow?
- Where do I belong?

- Who is walking with me?

Calling without capacity-building creates frustration. Over time, individuals either stagnate or seek fulfillment outside the church.

Capacity Without Calling Creates Burnout

Conversely, churches often rely on a small group of leaders who have developed capacity through years of service but are carrying more responsibility than intended. These leaders are capable, faithful, and committed but overextended.

When capacity is not replenished through generational development, burnout increases. Leaders remain in place not because they are called to, but because no one else has been prepared.

Leadership pipelines relieve this burden by distributing responsibility and cultivating future capacity.

What a Leadership Pipeline Is—and Is Not

A leadership pipeline is a structured yet relational process through which individuals move from participation to responsibility to leadership. It is not:
- A one-time training event
- A rigid hierarchy
- A replacement strategy
- A youth-only initiative

Instead, a leadership pipeline:
- Identifies potential early
- Develops leaders relationally
- Increases responsibility gradually
- Integrates mentoring and accountability
- Prepares leaders long before transition is needed

Pipelines honor both experience and emergence. They do not push leaders out; they prepare others to step in.

Biblical Roots of Leadership Pipelines

Scripture supports the idea of intentional leadership development. Moses prepared Joshua. Elijah formed Elisha. Jesus invested in the Twelve. Paul mentored Timothy. In each case, leadership was cultivated through time, trust, and responsibility.

These biblical examples reveal a consistent pattern:
1. Recognition of calling
2. Proximity and formation
3. Shared responsibility
4. Public affirmation
5. Gradual transition

This is the essence of a leadership pipeline.

Why Pipelines Are Especially Important Today

Cultural shifts, increased mobility, and changing expectations have made leadership continuity more challenging. Churches can no longer rely on longevity alone to sustain leadership. Intentional development is required.

Generational leadership pipelines provide:
- Stability during transition
- Clear expectations for growth
- Opportunities for collaboration
- Reduced conflict during change
- Long-term sustainability

Without pipelines, churches remain vulnerable to disruption and decline.

From Programs to Culture

The greatest mistake churches make is treating leadership development as a program rather than a culture. Programs can be added and removed. Culture shapes behavior over time.

Leadership pipelines function best when they are embedded in the life of the church integrated into worship, ministry teams, and decision-making processes.

When leadership development becomes part of the church's DNA, generational collaboration becomes normal rather than exceptional.

Section Summary

This section has argued that churches need leadership pipelines, not just passionate individuals. Calling must be matched with capacity, and capacity must be sustained through intentional development. Leadership pipelines provide the structure necessary for generational continuity, reducing burnout and preparing churches for faithful transition.

In the next section, we will explore how churches can identify emerging leaders across generations, moving from assumption to discernment.

Section 2

Identifying Emerging Leaders Across Generations: From Assumption to Discernment

One of the most common reasons leadership pipelines fail before they begin is that churches rely on assumption rather than discernment when identifying leaders. Too often, leadership potential is recognized only after individuals have already proven themselves through visible service, longevity, or proximity to power. While these indicators matter, they are incomplete.

Scripture presents leadership identification as a spiritual and communal process, not merely an observational one. When churches rush this process or neglect it altogether, they risk overlooking gifted leaders while overburdening those already in place.

The Myth of "Someone Will Step Up"

Many churches operate under the assumption that leadership will naturally emerge when needed. This belief is rooted in optimism, but it is rarely effective. Without intentional identification, leadership gaps are filled reactively rather than proactively.

When churches wait for someone to "step up," several things happen:
- Potential leaders hesitate, unsure if they are invited
- Leadership becomes associated with assertiveness rather than calling
- Quiet, gifted individuals are overlooked
- Crisis dictates leadership rather than formation

Discernment requires intentional attention long before leadership is urgently needed.

Biblical Discernment Versus Human Preference

Scripture repeatedly reminds us that God's criteria for leadership often differ from human expectations. God chose David while others overlooked him. Jesus called disciples who did not fit conventional leadership profiles. Paul invested in Timothy, who struggled with confidence and youthfulness.

These examples reveal that leadership discernment is not about surface qualifications alone. It involves prayer, observation, and spiritual attentiveness.

When churches identify leaders based solely on visibility, charisma, or familiarity, they limit the breadth of leadership God may be raising up.

Discernment Happens in Relationship

Leadership potential is most clearly discerned through **relationship and proximity**. Gifts emerge in community. Character is revealed over time. Calling is clarified through conversation and mentoring. Churches that rely only on formal nomination processes often miss these dynamics. Discernment requires leaders to know people beyond titles and roles to listen to their stories, observe their growth, and walk with them through challenge.

This relational discernment allows leadership identification to be both generous and grounded.

Looking Beyond One Generation

Intergenerational leadership pipelines require leaders to look beyond familiar age groups. Younger leaders may demonstrate initiative, creativity, and cultural fluency. Older leaders may show renewed calling, wisdom, and capacity for mentorship.

Leadership identification should not be limited by age assumptions. Scripture affirms both emerging and seasoned leadership when rooted in character and calling.

Churches that intentionally look across generations expand their leadership capacity and strengthen unity.

Signs of Emerging Leadership

While discernment is spiritual, it is not vague. Scripture and practice point to several indicators of emerging leadership:
- Teachability and humility
- Faithfulness in small responsibilities
- Willingness to serve without recognition
- Openness to feedback and growth
- Relational influence rather than positional authority

These qualities often appear before formal leadership roles are offered. Churches that train leaders to recognize these signs create healthier pipelines.

Creating Invitation, Not Pressure

Leadership identification should feel invitational, not coercive. Emerging leaders need permission to explore calling without fear of failure. Conversations should open doors, not impose expectations.

When leaders invite individuals into discernment rather than assigning them roles prematurely, they create space for prayerful clarity and shared understanding.

Section Summary

This section has emphasized that identifying leaders across generations requires intentional discernment rather than assumption. Leadership potential is revealed through relationship, character, and calling not merely visibility or longevity. Churches that recover discernment expand their leadership capacity and strengthen generational continuity.

In the next section, we will explore how churches can intentionally develop leaders through graduated responsibility, ensuring growth is sustainable and supported.

Section 3

Developing Leaders Through Graduated Responsibility

Once leaders are identified through prayerful discernment, the next critical question emerges: How are leaders formed? Too often, churches fall into one of two extremes. Either emerging leaders are placed into positions too quickly without adequate support, or they are held back indefinitely in the name of preparation. Both approaches undermine healthy leadership development.

Scripture points to a third way: graduated responsibility a process by which individuals are entrusted with increasing levels of responsibility over time, accompanied by mentoring, feedback, and accountability.

Formation Happens Through Responsibility

Leadership formation does not occur in abstraction. It happens through action. Scripture consistently shows that leaders grow by being entrusted with responsibility appropriate to their stage of development.

Jesus did not withhold mission from His disciples until they were fully formed. He sent them out, received them back, corrected them, and sent them again. Responsibility became the classroom.
Graduated responsibility allows leaders to learn through practice while remaining supported. Mistakes become moments of formation rather than sources of shame.

The Danger of Over-Promotion

When churches elevate leaders too quickly, often out of desperation or enthusiasm, they risk harming both the individual and the community. Over-promotion places pressure on emerging leaders before character and capacity have been sufficiently formed.

This can lead to burnout, discouragement, or public failure. In these cases, leadership development becomes associated with anxiety rather than growth.
Graduated responsibility protects against this by pacing development intentionally.

The Cost of Under-Utilization

At the opposite extreme, churches sometimes delay leadership development unnecessarily. Emerging leaders remain stuck in supporting roles long after they have demonstrated readiness for greater responsibility.

This delay often communicates distrust. Over time, capable leaders disengage or seek opportunities elsewhere. Under-utilization wastes gifts and weakens the pipeline.
Graduated responsibility ensures that leaders are neither rushed nor restrained.

Stages of Leadership Development

While each church context differs, leadership development often unfolds through identifiable stages:
1. Participation – Serving faithfully under direction
2. Assistance – Supporting leaders in shared tasks
3. Initiative – Leading with guidance and feedback
4. Ownership – Carrying responsibility with accountability
5. Multiplication – Developing others

These stages are not rigid, but they provide a framework for intentional growth. Leaders should know where they are and what comes next.

Mentoring and Feedback as Essential Supports

Graduated responsibility must be paired with mentoring and feedback. Responsibility without guidance leads to confusion. Guidance without responsibility leads to stagnation.

Effective mentoring provides:
- Regular reflection
- Honest evaluation
- Encouragement and correction
- Theological grounding
- Emotional support

Feedback ensures growth remains intentional and aligned with the church's mission.

Shared Leadership Builds Confidence

As responsibility increases, leaders should experience shared leadership rather than isolation. Emerging leaders should never feel they are carrying weight alone. Shared leadership models confidence and collaboration.

This approach also allows seasoned leaders to release responsibility gradually while remaining present and supportive.

Section Summary

This section has shown that leadership development flourishes through graduated responsibility. By pacing responsibility intentionally and pairing it with mentoring and feedback, churches create environments where leaders grow with confidence and integrity.

In the next section, we will explore how churches can create safe-to-learn environments, where mistakes are treated as formation rather than failure.

Section 4

Creating Safe-to-Learn Environments for Emerging Leaders

Leadership development cannot thrive in environments where mistakes are punished, questions are discouraged, or growth is equated with perfection. Churches that successfully cultivate leaders across generations intentionally create safe-to-learn environments spaces where individuals are encouraged to try, reflect, and grow under grace.

Scripture does not present leadership formation as error-free. It presents it as redemptive. Leaders grow not by avoiding mistakes, but by learning from them within supportive community.

Why Safety Matters in Leadership Formation

Safety in leadership development is not about lowering standards. It is about providing context for formation. Without safety, emerging leaders become risk averse. They avoid initiative, creativity, and responsibility.

In unsafe environments:
- Mistakes lead to embarrassment
- Feedback feels punitive
- Questions are interpreted as disloyalty
- Innovation is viewed with suspicion

These dynamics stifle growth and discourage generational engagement.

Biblical Precedent for Grace Filled Formation

Scripture offers numerous examples of leaders growing through failure. Peter denies Jesus yet becomes a foundational leader. The disciples misunderstand Jesus repeatedly yet are entrusted with the mission. Paul reflects openly on his past as part of his formation.

These narratives reveal that God forms leaders through grace, correction, and restoration. Churches that mirror this pattern create environments where leadership development is possible.

Distinguishing Failure from Faithlessness
One of the most damaging misconceptions in leadership culture is the belief that failure indicates disqualification. While Scripture takes sin seriously, it also affirms repentance and restoration.

Safe-to-learn environments distinguish between:
- Faithful mistakes made in growth
- Patterns of unrepentant behavior

This distinction allows churches to hold leaders accountable while still encouraging development.

Psychological and Relational Safety

Leadership formation requires psychological safety the confidence that one can speak, ask questions, and take initiative without fear of ridicule or reprisal. It also requires relational safety knowing that relationships will not be withdrawn after mistakes.

Churches cultivate this safety through:
- Clear expectations
- Consistent mentoring
- Private correction rather than public shaming
- Affirmation alongside feedback

When safety is present, leaders grow in confidence and maturity.

The Role of Senior Leaders in Modeling Safety

Senior leaders set the tone for leadership culture. When they acknowledge their own learning processes, mistakes, and growth, they normalize formation for others.

Modeling humility invites participation. Modeling grace encourages risk. Modeling accountability fosters trust.

Safe-to-learn environments begin at the top.

Balancing Safety and Responsibility

Safety does not eliminate responsibility. Emerging leaders must still meet expectations and grow in character. However, responsibility within a safe environment becomes formative rather than threatening. Clear boundaries, mentoring, and evaluation ensure that safety supports growth rather than excuses stagnation.

Section Summary

This section has emphasized that leadership development requires safe-to-learn environments where mistakes are treated as formation rather than failure. Grace-filled accountability allows leaders to grow with confidence and integrity, strengthening generational pipelines.

In the next section, we will explore how churches can institutionalize leadership development, ensuring pipelines endure beyond individual leaders or seasons.

Section 5

Institutionalizing Leadership Development for Long-Term Faithfulness

Leadership pipelines cannot depend solely on the vision, energy, or personality of a single pastor or leadership team. While strong leadership often initiates development, sustainability requires institutionalization the intentional embedding of leadership formation into the structures, rhythms, and expectations of the church.
Churches that fail to institutionalize leadership development often experience progress that is temporary. Momentum builds under a particular leader but dissipates when leadership changes or priorities shift. Pipelines collapse because they were never fully integrated into the life of the church.
Institutionalizing leadership development ensures that generational formation becomes a shared responsibility, not a personal project.

From Vision to Structure

Vision creates momentum, but structure sustains it. Churches that successfully develop leaders across generations translate theological conviction into practical systems that support formation over time.

Institutionalization does not mean bureaucracy. It means clarity. It means leadership development is:
- Expected, not optional
- Planned, not reactive
- Measured, not assumed
- Shared, not centralized

When leadership development is structurally supported, it becomes resilient rather than fragile.

Embedding Pipelines into Church Life

Leadership pipelines are most effective when they are integrated into existing ministries rather than operating as isolated programs. Formation should occur within:

- Ministry teams
- Worship leadership
- Teaching and discipleship environments
- Outreach and mission initiatives
- Decision-making processes

This integration ensures that leadership development feels natural rather than artificial. Leaders grow as they serve, reflect, and lead within the life of the church.

Creating Clear Expectations and Language

One of the key markers of institutionalized leadership development is shared language. Churches that develop leaders intentionally articulate clear expectations around growth, responsibility, and transition.
This clarity answers critical questions:
- How are leaders identified?
- What does growth look like?
- How is responsibility increased?
- How are leaders supported and evaluated?

Shared language reduces confusion and builds trust across generations.

Accountability Beyond Individuals

Institutionalization requires accountability structures that extend beyond individual leaders. Leadership development should be overseen by teams rather than dependent on a single advocate. When accountability is shared:
- Pipelines remain active during transitions
- Leaders are supported rather than isolated
- Evaluation becomes communal rather than personal
- Development remains aligned with mission

This shared accountability protects leadership pipelines from neglect or misuse.

Planning for Leadership Transition Before It Is

Needed

One of the most important functions of institutionalized pipelines is preparation for transition. Churches that plan proactively reduce fear and conflict when leadership changes occur.
Transition becomes an expected process rather than an emergency. Leaders step into new roles with confidence because formation has already taken place.
Succession, in this sense, becomes a celebration of faithfulness rather than a moment of crisis.

Leadership Development as a Measure of Health

Institutionalized leadership development becomes a key indicator of church health. Churches that consistently form leaders across generations demonstrate resilience, adaptability, and missional strength.

Rather than asking only how many attend or give, healthy churches also ask:
- Who is being developed?
- Who is being mentored?
- Who is being prepared to lead next?

These questions shift focus from maintenance to multiplication.

Section Summary

This section has argued that leadership pipelines must be institutionalized to endure. Vision initiates development, but structure sustains it. When leadership formation is embedded into church life, supported by shared accountability, and guided by clear expectations, generational continuity becomes possible.
In the final section of this chapter, we will draw these practices together and articulate a cohesive pipeline framework, summarizing how churches can move from calling to capacity with intention and faith.

Section 6

From Intention to Infrastructure: Preparing the Church for Generational Continuity

This chapter has argued that leadership development in the church must move beyond passion and potential into intentional infrastructure. Calling alone is not sufficient. Without clear pathways, mentorship, and accountability, even the most gifted individuals struggle to grow into faithful leaders.

Intergenerational leadership pipelines provide the structure through which calling becomes capacity and vision becomes sustainability. These pipelines honor both seasoned leaders and emerging ones by creating shared responsibility rather than competition, continuity rather than crisis.

The work of building pipelines is not about replacing leaders; it is about multiplying leadership. It is not about efficiency alone; it is about faithfulness over time.

Leadership Pipelines as Spiritual Formation

While this chapter has focused on structure, it must be emphasized that pipelines are not merely organizational tools. They are instruments of spiritual formation. Through discernment, graduated responsibility, mentoring, and accountability, leaders grow not only in skill, but in character and maturity.

Pipelines shape habits of humility, collaboration, and trust. They teach leaders to receive responsibility faithfully and to release it graciously. In this way, leadership development becomes discipleship in action.

Shared Ownership Across Generations

Healthy pipelines foster shared ownership of the church's mission. Older leaders are freed from the burden of carrying responsibility alone. Younger leaders are invited into meaningful participation. Middle generations become bridges rather than bottlenecks.

This shared ownership strengthens unity. When leadership development is transparent and intentional, suspicion decreases and trust grows. Transitions become anticipated rather than feared.

Preparing for What God Will Do Next

Churches that invest in leadership pipelines prepare themselves for God's future work. They remain flexible without losing theological integrity. They adapt without abandoning tradition. They grow without fragmenting.
Pipelines do not guarantee success, but they create readiness. They position the church to respond faithfully to new opportunities, challenges, and callings.

From Structure to Relationship

Leadership pipelines provide the framework, but relationships give them life. Without trust, dialogue, and mutual respect, even the best-designed pipelines fail.
The next chapter will focus on relational dynamics how churches can cultivate dialogue, trust, and shared vision across generations. Pipelines create pathways; relationships ensure those pathways are walked together.

Chapter 4 Summary

- Churches need leadership pipelines, not just passion
- Calling must be matched with capacity through structure
- Discernment identifies leaders; responsibility forms them
- Safe-to-learn environments sustain growth
- Institutionalization ensures longevity
- Pipelines prepare the church for generational continuity

CHAPTER 5
Generations in Dialogue: Moving from Tension to Trust

Section 1

Why Structures Fail Without Relationships

Churches can design thoughtful leadership pipelines, establish mentoring systems, articulate clear pathways for development—and still struggle to bridge generational divides. The reason is simple but profound: structures cannot replace relationships.

Leadership pipelines create opportunity, but relationships create trust. Without trust, structures feel imposed rather than invitational. Processes feel transactional rather than formative. Emerging leaders may move through stages yet still feel unseen. Seasoned leaders may release responsibility yet still feel disconnected.

Intergenerational leadership succeeds not merely when pathways exist, but when people feel heard, valued, and connected across generations.

The Relational Gap Beneath the Leadership Gap

Many generational leadership challenges are rooted less in policy than in perception. Younger leaders often perceive older leaders as resistant or controlling. Older leaders often perceive younger leaders as impatient or dismissive. These perceptions harden when generations do not share space for honest dialogue.

Without dialogue:
- Assumptions replace understanding
- Frustration replaces curiosity
- Silence replaces trust

Dialogue is not a luxury in generational leadership it is a necessity.

Dialogue as a Spiritual Practice

In Scripture, dialogue is central to formation. God speaks and listens. Jesus asks questions. The early church discerns together. Dialogue is not merely conversation; it is a spiritual practice that cultivates humility, patience, and mutual understanding.
Intergenerational dialogue invites leaders to listen not to respond, but to understand. It creates space for stories, fears, hopes, and convictions to be shared without immediate judgment.

When churches neglect dialogue, leadership development becomes mechanical. When they cultivate it, leadership becomes relational.

Why Generations Talk Past One Another

Generational tension often persists because groups speak from different experiences and assumptions. Older leaders speak from memory what the church has endured, preserved, and survived. Younger leaders speak from vision what the church could become, reach, and reimagine.

Both perspectives are valuable. Conflict arises when one is privileged over the other.
Dialogue allows memory and vision to meet not in competition, but in collaboration.

Listening as an Act of Leadership

One of the most transformative shifts a church can make is redefining leadership to include listening as action. Listening does not signal weakness; it demonstrates confidence and care.
When leaders listen across generations:
- Trust increases
- Fear decreases
- Misunderstanding is clarified
- Collaboration becomes possible

Listening affirms dignity. It communicates that voices matter even before decisions are made.

Creating Spaces for Honest Conversation

Dialogue does not happen automatically. Churches must intentionally create spaces where intergenerational conversation is encouraged and protected.

These spaces must be:
- Relational rather than performative
- Structured yet flexible
- Facilitated with humility
- Safe for honesty and disagreement

Without intentional spaces, dialogue remains superficial or sporadic.

Dialogue Precedes Delegation

One of the most common mistakes churches make is attempting to delegate responsibility before cultivating relationship. Authority given without dialogue often feels abrupt or artificial. Dialogue prepares hearts for shared leadership.

When generations understand one another, delegation becomes natural rather than threatening.

Section Summary

This section has argued that leadership structures cannot succeed without relational trust. Intergenerational dialogue is a spiritual practice that transforms tension into understanding and creates the foundation for shared leadership. Without dialogue, pipelines feel hollow. With it, they become pathways of unity.

In the next section, we will explore storytelling as a bridge between generations, examining how shared narratives create empathy, honor legacy, and shape shared vision.

Section 2

Storytelling as a Bridge Between Memory and Vision

Every church is shaped by stories. Some are celebrated publicly testimonies of faith, moments of sacrifice, seasons of growth. Others live quietly beneath the surface stories of struggle, conflict, resilience, and perseverance. Together, these narratives form the emotional and spiritual memory of a congregation.

Generational tension often intensifies when stories are not shared across age groups. Older generations carry memories that explain why certain decisions were made and why certain traditions matter. Younger generations carry questions shaped by present realities and future hopes. When these stories remain isolated, misunderstanding grows.

Storytelling functions as a bridge connecting memory and vision, past faithfulness and future calling.

Why Stories Matter More Than Strategies

Strategies organize ministry, but stories shape identity. People understand their place in the church not only through roles and policies, but through the narratives they hear and the experiences they inherit.

When churches neglect storytelling, younger leaders may interpret tradition as rigidity rather than resilience. Older leaders may interpret innovation as disrespect rather than responsibility. Stories provide context that strategies alone cannot.

Through storytelling, generations learn why the church believes what it believes and *how* it arrived where it is today.

Honoring Legacy Without Freezing the Past

Storytelling honors legacy by remembering God's faithfulness through specific people and moments. These stories deserve space, respect, and gratitude. However, when legacy is remembered without interpretation, it can unintentionally become restrictive.

Biblical memory is not about preserving the past unchanged; it is about remembering in order to move forward faithfully. Scripture repeatedly calls God's people to remember what God has done not to remain there, but to trust Him for what He will do next.

Healthy storytelling invites reflection rather than nostalgia. It honors the past while opening space for new chapters of faithfulness.

Creating Shared Narrative Across Generations

Shared narrative does not happen automatically. Churches must intentionally create opportunities for generations to tell and hear one another's stories.

This may include:
- Testimony gatherings across age groups
- Intergenerational small groups focused on faith stories
- Leadership retreats centered on shared history and future vision
- Structured storytelling moments in worship or teaching

These spaces allow generations to recognize one another not as obstacles, but as partners in a shared story.

Listening to Stories Builds Empathy

Storytelling requires attentive listening. When leaders listen to stories across generations, empathy grows. Younger leaders gain appreciation for sacrifice and perseverance. Older leaders gain insight into contemporary challenges and hopes.

Empathy transforms assumptions. What once felt like resistance may be revealed as concern. What once felt like impatience may be revealed as passion.

Empathy does not eliminate disagreement, but it changes how disagreement is handled.

Storytelling as Leadership Formation

Storytelling also forms leaders. Emerging leaders learn values, priorities, and theology through the lived experiences of those who came before them. Seasoned leaders rediscover purpose by seeing their legacy continue through others.
This reciprocal formation strengthens leadership continuity. Leaders are shaped not only by instruction, but by inheritance.

Moving from Individual Stories to Shared Vision

The ultimate goal of storytelling is not simply understanding it is alignment. When churches weave individual stories into a shared narrative, they create a foundation for collective vision.
Shared vision emerges when generations can say:
- "We know where we've been."
- "We understand where we are."
- "We agree on where God is leading us."

Storytelling prepares the soil for this shared commitment.

Section Summary

This section has shown that storytelling bridges generational divides by connecting memory and vision. Shared narratives foster empathy, honor legacy, and prepare the church for collective movement.
Without storytelling, dialogue remains shallow. With it, trust deepens and unity grows.
In the next section, we will explore how intentional listening practices deepen dialogue, moving beyond storytelling into sustained intergenerational engagement.

Section 3

Listening as a Discipline That Sustains Intergenerational Leadership

If dialogue opens the door and storytelling builds the bridge, listening is what allows people to cross it together. In many churches, listening is assumed rather than practiced. Leaders believe they are listening because conversations occur, meetings are held, and opinions are voiced. Yet true listening that transforms relationships and reshapes leadership culture requires intentional discipline.

Scripture presents listening not as passivity, but as obedience. "Let everyone be quick to listen, slow to speak, and slow to anger" is not merely relational advice; it is a leadership mandate. Listening forms humility, patience, and wisdom qualities essential for intergenerational collaboration.

The Difference Between Hearing and Listening

Hearing is passive; listening is active. Hearing acknowledges sound. Listening seeks understanding.
In generational contexts, leaders may hear concerns without fully engaging their meaning. Younger leaders may hear explanations of tradition without grasping the emotional weight behind them. Older leaders may hear calls for change without understanding the urgency driving them.
Listening requires leaders to ask not only what is being said, but why it matters.

Why Listening Often Breaks Down Across Generations

Listening breaks down when conversations feel unsafe, rushed, or performative. Generational conversations often carry emotional weight fear of loss, desire for recognition, concern for the church's future. When leaders listen defensively or selectively, trust erodes.

Common barriers to listening include:
- Preparing responses rather than attending fully
- Filtering feedback through assumptions
- Listening only to voices that affirm existing views
- Interpreting questions as challenges to authority

These patterns are rarely intentional, but they are deeply influential.

Listening as an Act of Trust

Listening communicates trust. It signals that another person's experience matters even when it differs from one's own. For emerging leaders, being listened to affirms belonging. For seasoned leaders, being listened to honors contribution and legacy.

Trust grows when leaders demonstrate consistency in listening not only during conflict, but in ordinary moments of ministry life.

Creating Rhythms of Listening

Listening becomes transformative when it is embedded into the rhythms of church life. One-time forums or listening sessions may initiate dialogue, but sustained change requires ongoing practice. Churches can cultivate listening through:
- Regular intergenerational roundtables
- Leadership meetings that prioritize reflection and dialogue
- Mentoring relationships centered on conversation
- Feedback loops that are acted upon, not ignored

These rhythms normalize listening as a leadership behavior rather than an exception.

Listening Without Immediate Resolution

One of the most challenging aspects of listening is resisting the urge to resolve quickly. Leaders often feel pressure to fix problems rather than understand them. Yet premature solutions can shut down dialogue. Listening without immediate resolution communicates patience and respect. It allows complexity to surface and invites collective discernment.

Scripture reminds leaders that wisdom often emerges through waiting, prayer, and shared reflection.

When Listening Leads to Change

Listening gains credibility when it leads to action. While not every concern results in immediate change, leaders must demonstrate that listening influences decision-making.
This does not require consensus on every issue. It requires transparency, explanation, and follow-through. When people see their voices shaping outcomes, trust deepens.

Listening Shapes Leadership Culture

Over time, intentional listening reshapes leadership culture. Conversations become more honest. Assumptions are challenged. Generational divides soften.
Listening does not eliminate disagreement, but it changes how disagreement is held. It allows leaders to disagree without disengaging and to differ without dividing.

Section Summary

This section has emphasized listening as a sustained leadership discipline essential for intergenerational trust. Listening moves dialogue from surface-level conversation to relational depth. When churches cultivate rhythms of listening, leadership pipelines gain relational strength and credibility.
In the next section, we will explore how collaboration across generations transforms leadership from parallel efforts into shared mission, completing the movement from dialogue to partnership.

Section 4

From Conversation to Collaboration: Leading Together Across Generations

Dialogue and listening, while essential, are not ends in themselves. Their purpose is to move the church toward collaboration, shared leadership rooted in trust, mutual respect, and common mission. When generations collaborate, leadership ceases to be a zero-sum game. It becomes a collective expression of faithfulness.

Collaboration transforms generational tension into generational strength. It allows the church to draw from memory and innovation, wisdom and creativity, experience and energy.

Why Collaboration Often Fails

Many churches attempt collaboration without first cultivating dialogue and trust. When collaboration is rushed, it feels forced. Younger leaders may feel tokenized. Older leaders may feel sidelined. Collaboration fails when:
- Authority is shared without relationship
- Roles are unclear
- Expectations are unspoken
- Power dynamics remain unaddressed

True collaboration requires intentional groundwork.

Collaboration Is Not Compromise

Collaboration is sometimes misunderstood as compromise each generation giving up something to keep the peace. In reality, collaboration seeks integration rather than concession.
Integration allows different perspectives to inform decisions without erasing distinct contributions. It honors both continuity and change.

Scripture presents collaboration as partnership in mission, not negotiation of preferences.

Shared Leadership as Mutual Submission

Biblical collaboration is grounded in mutual submission. Leaders submit not because they lack authority, but because they recognize God's work in others.

Mutual submission challenges hierarchical assumptions and invites humility. It allows leadership to be exercised collectively rather than competitively.

When generations practice mutual submission, authority becomes relational rather than positional.

Designing Collaborative Leadership Spaces

Collaboration does not occur spontaneously. Churches must intentionally design spaces where shared leadership is practiced. These spaces may include:
- Intergenerational leadership teams
- Co-teaching or co-preaching models
- Shared ministry planning sessions
- Joint decision-making bodies

Design matters. When collaborative spaces are clearly defined, participation feels meaningful rather than symbolic.

Clarifying Roles and Responsibilities

Effective collaboration requires clarity. Ambiguity breeds frustration. Leaders must know where authority resides, how decisions are made, and how accountability functions.

Clear roles allow collaboration to flourish without confusion or competition.

Clarity also protects relationships by reducing misunderstandings.

Learning Through Shared Work

Collaboration becomes formative when leaders learn together through shared work. Generations observe one another's strengths, problem solving approaches, and leadership styles.
Shared work fosters appreciation. Differences become assets rather than liabilities.
Through collaboration, leaders grow in trust and competence.

When Collaboration Builds Unity

Unity emerges not from agreement on every issue, but from commitment to shared mission. Collaboration anchors leaders to purpose rather than preference.

When generations lead together, the church experiences unity that is visible, resilient, and inspiring.

Section Summary

This section has shown that collaboration is the fruit of dialogue and listening. When churches design intentional spaces for shared leadership, clarify roles, and practice mutual submission, generational collaboration becomes a source of strength rather than tension.

In the final section of this chapter, we will draw these relational practices together and articulate a relational framework for intergenerational trust, preparing the reader for the book's concluding chapters.

Section 5

When Relationships Become the Pathway to Shared Leadership

This chapter has demonstrated that intergenerational leadership is sustained not merely by structure, but by relationship. Pipelines create opportunity, but trust determines whether those opportunities are embraced. Without dialogue, leadership development becomes mechanical. Without listening, collaboration becomes shallow. Without collaboration, generational unity remains aspirational rather than embodied.
Generational trust is not automatic, it is cultivated. It grows where leaders choose humility over assumption, curiosity over defensiveness, and relationship over efficiency.

Dialogue as the Soil of Trust

Dialogue provides the soil in which trust can grow. When generations are invited into honest conversation, they move beyond stereotypes and assumptions. Dialogue allows fear to be named, hopes to be shared, and misunderstandings to be clarified.

Churches that prioritize dialogue affirm that unity is not maintained by silence, but by truth spoken in love. This commitment creates relational depth that can sustain leadership transition and shared responsibility.

Storytelling as the Keeper of Memory and Vision

Storytelling anchors the church's identity. It honors the past without idolizing it and invites the future without dismissing legacy. When generations share stories, they discover that faithfulness did not begin with them and it will not end with them.

Shared narrative transforms "your vision" and "my memory" into our mission.

Listening as a Discipline of Love and Leadership

Listening has been framed in this chapter not as courtesy, but as discipline. Leaders who listen cultivate trust even when agreement is not immediate. Listening communicates dignity, value, and belonging.

When listening becomes habitual rather than occasional, leadership culture shifts. Disagreement no longer signals threat. Difference no longer signals division.

Collaboration as Embodied Unity

Collaboration represents the visible expression of generational trust. It is where dialogue becomes action and listening becomes shared leadership. When generations lead together, the church experiences unity that is practiced rather than proclaimed.
Collaboration does not erase difference it integrates it. It transforms diversity of experience into collective strength.

Relationships Prepare the Church for the Future

This chapter has shown that relational health is not optional for leadership continuity, it is essential. Churches that invest in dialogue, storytelling, listening, and collaboration prepare themselves for faithful transition and resilient mission.
When relationships are strong, change is navigable. When trust is present, leadership is shareable. When generations walk together, the church moves forward together.

Chapter 5 Summary

- Leadership structures require relational trust to function
- Dialogue transforms tension into understanding
- Storytelling bridges memory and vision

- Listening sustains trust across difference
- Collaboration embodies unity and shared mission
- Relationships make generational leadership possible

With theological foundations laid, barriers diagnosed, structures built, and relationships strengthened, the church is now positioned to move outward. The final chapters will focus on missional impact how generational leadership renewal strengthens witness, engages the community, and prepares the church for faithful presence in a changing world.

Chapter 6 will explore how intergenerational leadership fuels mission rather than distraction, demonstrating that leadership continuity is not about survival, but about gospel faithfulness.

CHAPTER 6
From Continuity to Commission: Generational Leadership and the Mission of the Church

Section 1

Why Generational Leadership Is a Missional Issue, Not an Internal One

For many churches, conversations about generational leadership are treated as internal matters questions of governance, staffing, or succession. While these elements are important, they do not capture the full theological weight of the issue. Generational leadership is not merely about who leads next; it is about how faithfully the church bears witness to the gospel across time.

When leadership continuity is weak, mission suffers. When leadership renewal is strong, witness expands.
Scripture consistently presents leadership as a means toward God's redemptive purposes in the world. Leadership exists not for self-preservation, but for proclamation, service, and discipleship. Therefore, generational leadership must be understood as a missional issue, deeply connected to the church's calling to make Christ known.

Mission Depends on Continuity

The mission of the church is long-term by design. The Great Commission assumes generational faithfulness teaching, baptizing, and forming disciples who will do the same. This work cannot be sustained if leadership is concentrated within a single generation or disrupted by poorly prepared transitions.

When churches fail to develop leaders across generations, mission becomes episodic rather than enduring. Outreach initiatives start and stop. Vision resets repeatedly. Momentum is lost.

Generational leadership continuity provides stability that allows mission to mature rather than restart.

The Watching World and Leadership Credibility

Churches do not lead in isolation. Communities observe how churches treat their leaders, navigate change, and handle difference. When leadership transitions are marked by conflict, secrecy, or collapse, credibility erodes not only internally, but externally.

Conversely, when generations lead together with humility and trust, the church embodies the reconciling power of the gospel. Intergenerational leadership becomes a living testimony of unity in Christ.

The church's witness is strengthened when leadership reflects the gospel it proclaims.

Missional Blind Spots Created by Generational Disconnect

Generational disconnect creates missional blind spots. When leadership lacks generational diversity, churches may struggle to understand the communities they serve. Cultural shifts go unnoticed. Emerging needs remain unmet. Language, platforms, and engagement strategies lag behind reality.
Intergenerational leadership broadens perspective. Younger leaders often bring cultural awareness and innovative approaches. Older leaders bring theological depth and institutional wisdom. Together, they enable the church to engage the world faithfully and intelligently. Mission thrives where generations collaborate.

Leadership Renewal and Gospel Transmission

The gospel is always transmitted through people. Faith is taught, modeled, and embodied. Leadership renewal ensures that the gospel is not only preserved doctrinally but lived relationally.

When younger leaders are formed within the community of faith, they inherit not only beliefs, but practices and values. When older leaders invest relationally, they pass on wisdom rather than merely information.

This relational transmission strengthens the church's missional identity.

From Maintenance to Movement

Churches that neglect generational leadership often drift into maintenance mode. Energy is spent sustaining programs rather than advancing mission. Fear of change replaces expectation of growth.

Generational leadership renewal reorients the church toward movement. It shifts focus from what must be preserved to what God is calling forth next.

Movement requires leaders who are formed, trusted, and empowered across generations.

Section Summary

This section has argued that generational leadership is a missional issue at its core. Leadership continuity sustains mission, strengthens witness, and expands the church's capacity to engage the world faithfully. When generations lead together, the church moves from maintenance to movement.
In the next section, we will explore how intergenerational leadership shapes discipleship and outreach, demonstrating that leadership renewal directly influences how the church forms disciples and serves its community.

Section 2

How Intergenerational Leadership Strengthens Discipleship and Outreach

Discipleship and outreach are often discussed as programs or initiatives, but Scripture presents them as relational processes rooted in leadership example. How leaders are formed, supported, and shared across generations profoundly influences how disciples are made and how the church engages the world.
Intergenerational leadership renewal does not distract from discipleship and outreach it deepens them.

Discipleship Is Modeled Before It Is Taught

Discipleship is learned as much by observation as by instruction. When believers see leaders across generations serving, listening, and learning together, they witness discipleship in action.
Intergenerational leadership models:
- Humility across difference
- Mutual submission
- Faithfulness over time
- Respect for wisdom and innovation

These visible practices teach disciples how to live their faith in community.

Leadership Diversity Expands Discipleship Pathways

When leadership reflects generational diversity, discipleship pathways multiply. Younger believers see accessible role models. Older believers find renewed purpose in mentoring and formation.

Discipleship becomes less about information transfer and more about relational growth. Faith is no longer perceived as generationally siloed but as a shared journey.

This shared journey strengthens retention and engagement across age groups.

Outreach Requires Generational Awareness

Effective outreach depends on understanding the community being served. Generationally diverse leadership equips churches to engage a wider range of people with cultural sensitivity and relevance.

Younger leaders often recognize emerging needs, platforms, and communication styles. Older leaders offer discernment, stability, and long-term perspective. Together, they help the church remain faithful without becoming outdated.
Outreach thrives when leadership is both rooted and responsive.

Intergenerational Leadership as a Witness to Reconciliation

In a polarized world marked by division and generational mistrust, churches that embody intergenerational leadership offer a powerful witness. Collaboration across age, experience, and perspective reflects the reconciling work of Christ.
This visible unity speaks louder than strategy. It demonstrates that the gospel has the power to bring diverse people into shared mission.

Outreach becomes credible when the church practices what it proclaims.

Passing Faith, Not Just Programs

One of the greatest dangers in ministry is mistaking activity for formation. Programs may engage temporarily, but faith is sustained relationally.

Intergenerational leadership ensures that discipleship is passed through relationships rather than merely through curriculum. Wisdom is shared, questions are welcomed, and faith is contextualized.

This relational passing of faith strengthens spiritual maturity and resilience.

Discipleship That Prepares Leaders

Discipleship and leadership development are inseparable. Discipleship that does not prepare believers for responsibility limits growth. Leadership renewal ensures discipleship leads toward service and stewardship.

As disciples grow, they are invited into leadership formation not abruptly, but intentionally. This integration strengthens both discipleship and leadership pipelines.

Section Summary

This section has shown that intergenerational leadership strengthens discipleship and outreach by modeling faith, expanding pathways, and enhancing cultural engagement. Leadership renewal deepens the church's ability to form disciples and serve its community faithfully.

In the next section, we will examine how generational leadership prepares the church for future challenges, ensuring mission remains resilient amid cultural and organizational change.

Section 3

Preparing the Church for a Changing World Through Generational Leadership

The church does not exist in a static environment. Cultural shifts, technological change, social upheaval, and evolving community needs continually reshape the context in which ministry takes place. Churches that fail to prepare for these changes often find themselves reacting rather than discerning, preserving structures rather than pursuing mission.
Generational leadership renewal prepares the church not merely to survive change, but to faithfully engage it.

Change Is Inevitable; Unfaithfulness Is Not

Scripture reminds us that while the message of the gospel remains constant, the contexts in which it is proclaimed do not. God's people have always had to discern how to live faithfully in new seasons.

Generational leadership allows churches to respond to change without abandoning conviction. Younger leaders often recognize cultural shifts early. Older leaders provide theological grounding and historical perspective. Together, they help the church adapt wisely rather than impulsively.

Faithfulness is preserved not by resisting change, but by engaging it prayerfully.

Building Adaptive Capacity Through Shared Leadership

Adaptive capacity refers to a church's ability to respond to new challenges with resilience and creativity. Churches with generationally diverse leadership develop greater adaptive capacity because they draw from a broader range of experiences and perspectives.

Shared leadership reduces dependence on a single voice or approach. It encourages experimentation while maintaining accountability. When one generation struggles to interpret a new reality, another may offer insight.

Adaptive capacity is strengthened when leadership is collaborative.

Preparing Leaders for Challenges Not Yet Seen

One of the most important functions of leadership development is preparation for challenges that cannot yet be named. Cultural conversations, ethical dilemmas, and community needs will continue to evolve.

Generational leadership pipelines prepare leaders not by predicting the future, but by forming leaders who can discern faithfully in uncertainty. These leaders are grounded in Scripture, shaped by community, and open to learning.

Formation, not foresight, is the key to future readiness.

Resilience Through Intergenerational Support

Leadership can be isolating, particularly during seasons of rapid change. Intergenerational leadership creates networks of support that strengthen resilience.

Younger leaders benefit from mentorship during uncertainty. Older leaders find encouragement in shared responsibility. Together, leaders are less likely to burn out or withdraw.
Resilient leadership sustains mission through adversity.

Avoiding the Trap of Nostalgia or Novelty

Churches unprepared for change often fall into one of two traps: nostalgia or novelty. Nostalgia idealizes the past and resists adaptation. Novelty chases relevance without discernment.
Generational leadership offers a corrective to both extremes. Memory and innovation are held in tension. The church remembers where God has been faithful while remaining attentive to where God is leading.

This balance allows the church to remain rooted and responsive.

Leadership Renewal as Ongoing Practice

Future readiness is not achieved through a single initiative. It is sustained through ongoing leadership renewal. Churches that regularly develop leaders across generations remain open to God's future work.

Leadership renewal becomes part of the church's spiritual rhythm an expression of trust that God's mission continues beyond any one season or leader.

Section Summary

This section has shown that generational leadership prepares the church for a changing world by strengthening adaptive capacity, resilience, and discernment. Leadership renewal enables the church to remain faithful amid uncertainty, avoiding the traps of nostalgia and novelty.

In the next section, we will explore how generational leadership shapes the church's long-term witness, drawing together mission, formation, and hope for the future.

Section 4

Generational Leadership and the Church's Enduring Witness

The church's witness is not measured solely by what it accomplishes in a single season, but by what it faithfully hands forward over time. Scripture consistently frames God's work as generational rooted in remembrance, obedience, and hope. Leadership, therefore, plays a central role in shaping not only what the church does, but how it is remembered.
Generational leadership renewal ensures that the church's witness endures beyond personalities, programs, and particular moments of success.

Witness as Faithfulness Over Time

Biblical witness is cumulative. It is built through consistent obedience, lived example, and transmitted faith. Churches that invest in leadership across generations demonstrate that the gospel is not dependent on a single leader or era.
This long view of witness resists the pressure to measure success only by immediate results. Instead, it emphasizes faithfulness trusting that God works through generations to accomplish His purposes.

Generational leadership aligns the church's vision with God's redemptive timeline.

Leadership as Public Theology

How the church forms, shares, and transitions leadership communicates theology publicly. Leadership practices reveal what the church believes about power, authority, community, and trust.
When leadership is guarded, exclusive, or fear-driven, it communicates a theology of scarcity. When leadership is shared, formed, and entrusted, it communicates a theology of abundance and grace.

The church's witness is strengthened when leadership practices reflect the gospel it proclaims.

Intergenerational Unity as Missional Testimony

In a world increasingly marked by division generational, cultural, political the church has an opportunity to embody a different reality. Intergenerational leadership offers a visible testimony of reconciliation.

When generations serve, decide, and lead together, the church demonstrates that unity in Christ transcends difference. This embodied unity invites curiosity and credibility.

The gospel is not only heard it is seen.

Legacy as Stewardship, Not Control

Legacy is often misunderstood as preserving influence or maintaining personal imprint. Scripture presents legacy as stewardship entrusting what has been received to others faithfully.

Generational leadership reframes legacy from control to contribution. Leaders leave not by holding on longer, but by preparing others well.

This stewardship-focused legacy frees leaders to serve joyfully rather than defensively.

Witness Beyond the Church Walls

The church's internal leadership culture shapes its external reputation. Communities notice whether churches empower younger voices, honor elders, and navigate change with integrity.

Churches that practice generational leadership renewal are better positioned to partner with their communities, speak prophetically, and serve humbly.

Leadership continuity enhances credibility.

Hope Rooted in God's Faithfulness

Ultimately, generational leadership is an expression of hope. It declares confidence that God's work continues beyond any one leader or generation. It affirms that the same God who was faithful in the past will remain faithful in the future.

This hope sustains leaders through transition and prepares the church to face the unknown with trust.

Section Summary

This section has shown that generational leadership shapes the church's enduring witness by aligning leadership practices with gospel values, strengthening unity, and reframing legacy as stewardship. When leadership is entrusted across generations, the church's witness becomes resilient and credible.

In the final section of this chapter, we will draw these missional insights together and issue a call to faithful action, preparing the reader for the book's concluding chapter.

Section 5

Leadership Renewal as an Act of Missional

Faithfulness

This chapter has argued that generational leadership is not a peripheral concern, but a missional imperative. Leadership continuity sustains the church's ability to bear witness faithfully across time. Without intentional renewal, mission becomes fragile, dependent on individuals rather than rooted in community.

Generational leadership renewal positions the church to live out the Great Commission with integrity, resilience, and hope.

Leadership as a Means, Not an End

Throughout this book, leadership has been framed not as an end in itself, but as a means toward God's redemptive purposes. Leaders exist to equip the body, to model discipleship, and to extend the church's witness.

When leadership becomes self-protective or insular, mission narrows. When leadership is entrusted and shared, mission expands.

Leadership renewal keeps the church oriented outward.

Mission Thrives Where Leadership Is Shared

This chapter has shown that mission is strengthened when leadership is generationally diverse and collaborative. Discipleship deepens. Outreach becomes more responsive. The church's witness grows more credible.

Shared leadership reflects trust in God's ongoing work through the whole body of Christ. It affirms that the Spirit equips believers across generations for service and witness.

Faithfulness Across Seasons

Generational leadership renewal affirms that the church's calling extends beyond any one season. Faithfulness is measured not by longevity of control, but by willingness to prepare others.

This perspective frees leaders to serve with joy rather than fear. It invites the church to view transition as testimony rather than threat.

Hope That Looks Forward

At its core, generational leadership is an expression of hope. It declares that God's mission continues, that the gospel remains powerful, and that the church is not bound by its past.
Hope empowers leaders to act courageously, invest relationally, and trust the Spirit's work beyond their own tenure.

Chapter 6 Summary

- Generational leadership is a missional issue
- Leadership continuity sustains witness
- Shared leadership strengthens discipleship and outreach
- Intergenerational collaboration prepares the church for change
- Leadership renewal shapes enduring witness
- Hope in God's faithfulness anchors transition

The journey through theology, diagnosis, structure, relationship, and mission now leads to a final question: What is required of us now? The final chapter will invite pastors, leaders, and congregations to reflect personally and collectively on their role in generational faithfulness. The book will conclude with a call to commitment not merely to strategies, but to a posture of stewardship, trust, and obedience.

CHAPTER 7
Faithful Stewards of What We Have Received

Section 1

Standing at the Threshold of Generational Responsibility

Every generation of the church eventually arrives at a defining moment, a threshold where it must decide whether it will simply preserve what it has inherited or faithfully steward it for those who will come next. This book has traced the theological foundations, named the obstacles, offered practical pathways, and explored the relational and missional implications of generational leadership. Now, the question becomes unavoidable: What will we do with what we know?

Generational leadership is not ultimately about strategy or succession. It is about stewardship. It asks leaders to hold the past with gratitude, the present with courage, and the future with trust in God.

What We Have Received Is Not Ours to Keep

Scripture consistently frames leadership as something received rather than possessed. Faith, authority, wisdom, and responsibility are entrusted not owned. They are meant to be cultivated, shared, and passed on.

This truth challenges deeply held assumptions about leadership permanence and control. Leaders are not called to secure their place, but to prepare others. Churches are not called to freeze faith in a particular form, but to transmit it faithfully across time.

To receive without passing on is to misunderstand the nature of stewardship.

The Weight of Faithful Inheritance

What has been inherited carries weight. Churches today stand on the prayers, sacrifices, and faithfulness of those who came before. Their labor made worship, ministry, and witness possible.

Honoring that inheritance does not mean preserving every practice unchanged. It means discerning how to steward the heart of that faithfulness in new contexts. Inheritance becomes most meaningful when it is activated rather than archived.
Faithful stewardship respects the past while preparing the future.

The Cost of Avoiding the Question

Avoiding generational responsibility comes at a cost. Leadership gaps widen. Trust erodes. Mission narrows. The church remains active but increasingly fragile.

This cost is rarely immediate, which makes avoidance tempting. Yet Scripture warns that delayed obedience often produces diminished fruit.

Generational leadership renewal invites courage not because the outcome is guaranteed, but because obedience is required.

Leadership Begins with Personal Resolve

Before structures are built or conversations are held, generational leadership begins with personal resolve. Leaders must decide:
- To release fear
- To listen intentionally
- To invest relationally
- To act courageously

This resolve is not rooted in confidence in self, but in trust in God's ongoing work.

The Invitation to Faithful Stewardship

This final chapter is an invitation not an indictment. It invites leaders to reflect honestly on where they stand and how they will respond. It invites churches to embrace generational leadership as a spiritual calling rather than an organizational task.

Faithful stewardship is not about doing everything perfectly. It is about walking obediently, trusting that God honors faithfulness across generations.

Section Summary

This opening section of the final chapter has reframed generational leadership as stewardship and responsibility. What has been received must be entrusted forward. Avoidance carries cost, but obedience invites hope. Leadership renewal begins with personal and communal resolve.

In the next section, we will explore what faithful stewardship looks like in practice, naming concrete commitments leaders and churches can make as they move forward.

Section 2

Commitments That Turn Conviction into Faithful Action

Conviction without commitment rarely produces change. Many leaders agree with the need for generational leadership renewal yet struggle to translate that agreement into sustained action. This gap between belief and behavior is not caused by apathy, but by uncertainty leaders are unsure where to begin or what faithfulness requires of them personally.

Faithful stewardship becomes tangible when conviction is anchored to clear commitments. These commitments do not demand perfection, but they do require intentionality, courage, and consistency.

A Commitment to Examine Leadership Practices Honestly

The first act of faithful stewardship is honest examination. Churches must be willing to ask difficult questions about how leadership is currently practiced.

This examination includes asking:
- Who holds influence and why?
- Whose voices are heard consistently?
- How are leaders identified and developed?
- Where are generational gaps most visible?

Honest examination is not about blame it is about clarity. Without clarity, change remains superficial.

A Commitment to Share Authority, Not Just Responsibility

One of the most challenging commitments leaders face is the willingness to share authority rather than merely assign tasks.

Delegating responsibility without authority limits growth and reinforces hierarchy.
Faithful stewardship invites leaders to trust others with real decision-making power—appropriately, gradually, and relationally. This trust affirms calling and builds confidence across generations.

Shared authority reflects confidence in God's work beyond oneself.

A Commitment to Invest Relationally, Not Transactionally

Leadership development is not efficient. It requires time, patience, and presence. Faithful stewardship resists the temptation to treat people as resources rather than relationships.

This commitment involves:
- Mentoring intentionally
- Listening consistently
- Walking alongside emerging leaders through uncertainty
- Valuing presence over productivity

Relational investment creates leaders who are formed, not merely functional.

A Commitment to Courageous Conversation

Avoidance is easier than honesty, but faithful stewardship requires courageous conversation. Leaders must be willing to address tension, name fear, and engage difference with grace.
This commitment includes creating space for dialogue across generations and modeling how to disagree without dividing.
Courageous conversation protects unity by grounding it in truth.

A Commitment to Long-Term Formation

Leadership renewal is not a quick fix. It is a long-term practice that unfolds over seasons. Faithful stewardship resists impatience and embraces formation over time.

This commitment acknowledges that some fruit will be harvested later, perhaps by others. Leaders act faithfully even when immediate results are unseen.

A Commitment to Trust God's Ongoing Work

At the heart of generational leadership is trust trust that God continues to call, equip, and send leaders beyond one's own tenure. Faithful stewardship rests not in control, but in confidence that God is faithful to His church.
This trust frees leaders to release fear and embrace hope.

Section Summary

This section has named key commitments that turn conviction into faithful action. Honest examination, shared authority, relational investment, courageous conversation, long-term formation, and trust in God form the foundation of generational stewardship.

In the next section, we will address the cost and courage of letting go, exploring what leaders must release in order to entrust faithfully.

Section 3

The Courage to Release What God Never Intended Us to Keep

For many leaders, the most painful part of generational stewardship is not building or investing it is letting go. Release feels like loss. It stirs fear of irrelevance, grief over changing seasons, and uncertainty about what comes next. Even faithful leaders can struggle here, not because they lack trust in God, but because leadership is deeply intertwined with identity.
Yet Scripture is clear: what God entrusts to us is never meant to terminate with us.

Letting Go Is Not Abandonment

One of the greatest misconceptions about release is the belief that it equals abandonment. In reality, release is not stepping away from responsibility, it is stepping into a new expression of faithfulness.

Biblical leaders did not disappear after releasing responsibility. Moses remained present even after Joshua was commissioned. Elijah continued to walk with Elisha before ascending. Paul stayed connected to Timothy through letters, counsel, and prayer.

Release is not withdrawal; it is **repositioning**.

Why Release Feels So Threatening

Release threatens the parts of leadership that feel safest:
- Familiar routines
- Established influence
- Clear identity
- Predictable authority

Leadership seasons give structure to our sense of purpose. When seasons shift, leaders may ask quietly:
- Who am I if I am no longer in this role?
- Will my voice still matter?
- Will what I built be honored?

These questions are not signs of weakness they are invitations to deeper trust.

Scripture's Pattern of Faithful Release

Throughout Scripture, God consistently calls leaders to release before they feel ready. Abraham leaves what is familiar. Moses hands authority to Joshua. Jesus entrusts the mission to imperfect disciples.

Release precedes multiplication.

God often does His greatest work after leaders release control, not before. What feels like loss becomes the soil of fruitfulness.

Release as an Act of Worship

At its core, release is worship. It declares that leadership belongs to God, not to us. It affirms that God's purposes are larger than our tenure and stronger than our grip.
When leaders release authority prayerfully, they offer their work back to God. This surrender honors God's sovereignty and affirms faith in His ongoing work.

Making Room for Others to Rise

Holding on too tightly, even with good intentions, limits space for others to grow. Emerging leaders need room to make decisions, learn, and lead authentically.

Release creates space not for chaos, but for formation. It allows others to step forward with confidence rather than hesitation.
This is how leadership multiplies rather than stagnates.

Redefining Legacy Through Release

Legacy is often misunderstood as being remembered for what one controlled or built. Scripture redefines legacy as what continues after one release.

Leaders who release faithfully are remembered not for dominance, but for generosity. Not for longevity, but for impact.
Legacy rooted in release is resilient because it belongs to God.

Section Summary

This section has explored the courage required to release leadership as an act of faithful stewardship. Release is not abandonment or loss it is worship, trust, and obedience. Scripture affirms that God multiplies what leaders are willing to entrust.

In the next section, we will explore how leaders can remain meaningfully engaged after release, reframing presence, mentorship, and purpose in new seasons.

Section 4

Remaining Present Without Standing in the Way

One of the unspoken fears surrounding leadership transition is the belief that release requires disappearance. Leaders worry that stepping aside means stepping out that their voice, wisdom, and presence will no longer matter. Scripture, however, offers a richer vision of leadership after transition, one marked not by control, but by continued contribution.
Faithful release does not end calling; it reshapes it.

Presence Without Possession

Healthy generational leadership distinguishes between presence and possession. Leaders can remain present without possessing authority. They can offer wisdom without directing outcomes. They can support without overshadowing.
This posture requires humility and discernment. It asks leaders to shift from being the primary decision-maker to being a trusted guide, available, attentive, and respectful of new leadership's space.

Presence without possession builds confidence rather than competition.

Scripture's Model of Post-Transition Leadership

Scripture provides multiple examples of leaders remaining meaningfully engaged after releasing authority. Moses continued to intercede for the people even after Joshua assumed leadership. Elijah walked alongside Elisha until his departure. Paul maintained pastoral oversight through encouragement, prayer, and counsel.

These leaders did not cling to control, nor did they withdraw into silence. They occupied a supportive, affirming role, allowing new leaders to grow while remaining rooted in relationship.

The Ministry of Affirmation

One of the most powerful contributions leaders can make after release is affirmation. Public support communicates trust. Private encouragement sustains confidence. Silence, when interpreted as withdrawal or resentment, can undermine emerging leadership.

Affirmation does not require agreement on every decision. It requires commitment to unity, growth, and shared mission.
When leaders affirm rather than critique from the sidelines, they strengthen the church's leadership culture.

Mentorship Without Micromanagement

Post-transition leadership often takes the form of mentorship. However, mentorship must be practiced carefully. Guidance that feels like oversight can quickly become interference.

Healthy mentorship:
- Is invited rather than imposed
- Listen before advising
- Honors new leadership authority
- Offers wisdom without expectation of compliance

Mentorship thrives when trust replaces control.

Navigating the Emotional Work of Transition

Remaining present without standing in the way requires emotional maturity. Leaders must process grief, identity shifts, and changing rhythms. These emotions are natural and deserve acknowledgment.

Churches can support this work by honoring outgoing leaders publicly, providing space for reflection, and affirming ongoing values beyond formal roles.

When emotional work is neglected, resentment can quietly take root.

Redefining Influence

Influence does not disappear with position, it changes shape. Leaders continue to influence through example, encouragement, prayer, and relational presence.
This redefinition frees leaders to serve joyfully rather than defensively. It allows them to witness the fruit of their investment without needing to control it.

Section Summary

This section has reframed leadership after release as a season of meaningful presence rather than absence. Scripture affirms that leaders can remain engaged without hindering growth. Presence without possession, affirmation without control, and mentorship without micromanagement create environments where generational leadership flourishes.
In the final section of this chapter and the book we will offer a commissioning call, inviting leaders and churches to step forward in hope, trust, and obedience.

Section 5

A Commission to Lead Faithfully Across Generations

This book began with a question that now becomes a calling: Will we steward what we have received, or will we merely preserve it?
Scripture leaves little ambiguity. What God entrusts to one generation is always intended for the next. Faithfulness is measured not by how long we hold on, but by how well we prepare others to carry the work forward.
Generational leadership is not a trend to be adopted or resisted. It is a sacred responsibility rooted in the character of God Himself the God of Abraham, Isaac, and Jacob; the God who works across generations to fulfill His redemptive purposes.

A Call to Faithful Obedience

Leaders are now invited to respond not merely with agreement, but with obedience. Obedience may look like difficult conversations, intentional investment, courageous release, or renewed trust in God's ongoing work. It may require letting go of comfort and certainty in order to embrace faithfulness.
Obedience rarely feels efficient. It often feels risky. Yet Scripture affirms that God honors obedience that is grounded in trust.

A Commission to Churches

To churches, this work issues a clear commission:
Create space for generations to lead together.
Honor the past without idolizing it.
Embrace the future without fearing it.
Invest relationally, not just structurally.
Trust the Spirit to guide the work beyond human control.
When churches embrace this commission, leadership renewal becomes an act of worship and mission rather than anxiety and survival.

A Commission to Leaders

To leaders, especially those who have carried weight faithfully for many years, this book offers affirmation and invitation. Your labor has mattered. Your faithfulness has borne fruit. Now you are invited into the holy work of entrustment preparing others to lead with integrity, courage, and humility.
Leadership does not end with release. It multiplies through it.

A Commission to Emerging Leaders

To emerging leaders, this book offers encouragement and responsibility. You are not an interruption to the church's story—you are part of its continuation. Your voice matters. Your calling is real. Your training is sacred.
Honor those who have gone before you. Learn deeply. Lead humbly. Serve faithfully.

Trusting the God Who Holds the Generations

At the center of this work stands a profound truth: **the church does not belong to us**. It belongs to God. The same God who was faithful in the past will remain faithful in the future.
Generational leadership renewal rests not in perfect plans, but in confident trust that God continues to call, equip, and send His people.

Final Word

May churches who engage this work become places where faith is passed on with integrity, leadership is shared with trust, and mission is pursued with courage. May leaders steward their influence with humility and hope. May generations walk together not in fear of change, but in confidence in God's faithfulness.

The work continues. The call remains. The generations await.

About the Author

Dr. K. A. "Shawn" Dooley is a pastor, preacher, Army veteran, and theological educator committed to helping churches steward leadership faithfully across generations. He serves in Central Texas, where his ministry focuses on biblical preaching, leadership development, pastoral care, and strengthening congregations for long-term faithfulness and mission.

Dr. Dooley holds two doctoral degrees a Doctor of Ministry (DMin) and a Doctor of Theology (ThD) and brings together rigorous theological scholarship with lived pastoral experience. His academic training is complemented by the completion of multiple units of Clinical Pastoral Education (CPE), equipping him to provide compassionate pastoral care in clinical, congregational, and community settings.

A United States Army veteran, Dr. Dooley's leadership is shaped by discipline, service, and a deep commitment to people under pressure. His military background, combined with pastoral ministry and clinical training, informs his approach to leadership, stewardship, and resilience in the life of the church.

Dr. Dooley has extensive experience guiding churches through leadership formation, generational transition, and community engagement. He is passionate about mentoring emerging leaders while honoring the wisdom and faithfulness of those who have served before them. His preaching and writing reflect a deep love for the church and a conviction that leadership must be entrusted, not merely preserved.

Faithful Across Generations grows out of both scholarly research and lived ministry experience. Through this work, Dr. Dooley seeks to encourage pastors, ministry leaders, and congregations to honor the past, engage the present, and prepare the future together.

Faithful Across Generations Church & Leadership Study Guide

Purpose of This Guide

This study guide is designed to help churches, leadership teams, and ministry cohorts engage the themes of *Faithful Across Generations* in thoughtful, prayerful, and practical ways. The goal is not simply discussion, but discernment and action helping leaders steward faith, authority, and mission across generations.

This guide may be used in:
- Leadership retreats
- Pastor and staff development
- Deacon / board training
- Intergenerational small groups
- Seminary or Ministry Cohorts

Each chapter includes Scripture, reflection, discussion, and action steps to move learning into faithful practice.

How to Use This Guide

Each session is designed for 60–90 minutes and includes:
1. Key Theme
2. Scripture Focus
3. Summary Reflection
4. Discussion Questions
5. Leadership Reflection
6. Action Step

Leaders are encouraged to create space for honest dialogue, listening, and prayer.

CHAPTER 1 STUDY

Why Generational Leadership Matters Biblically

Key Theme
Faithfulness is designed to be passed on, not assumed.
Scripture Focus
- Deuteronomy 6:4–9
- **Psalm 78:4–7**

Summary Reflection
Scripture consistently frames faith as something that must be intentionally taught, modeled, and entrusted. Leadership is part of this calling. When leadership formation is neglected, faith transmission becomes fragile.

Discussion Questions
1. How has leadership traditionally been passed on in our church?
2. Where do we assume faithfulness without intentionally forming it?
3. What biblical images of generational faith stand out most to you?

Leadership Reflection
What practices in my leadership help pass faith forward? What practices unintentionally keep it centralized?

Action Step
Identify one way your church can intentionally teach leadership across generations this year.

CHAPTER 2 STUDY

A Biblical Theology of Leadership Across Generations

Key Theme
Leadership is stewardship, not ownership.

Scripture Focus
- Numbers 27:18–23
- 2 Timothy 2:1–2
-

Summary Reflection
Biblical leadership involves entrustment. God calls leaders not to preserve authority indefinitely, but to prepare others faithfully.

Discussion Questions
1. How do we define leadership authority in our context?
2. What fears arise when we talk about releasing authority?
3. How does Scripture challenge modern leadership assumptions?

Leadership Reflection
Where might I be holding responsibility that God is calling me to entrust?

Action Step
Create a mentoring or apprenticeship relationship between leaders of different generations.

CHAPTER 3 STUDY

Why Churches Struggle to Change What They Can Clearly See

Key Theme
Knowing the problem does not automatically produce change.

Scripture Focus
- Matthew 23:23–28
- James 1:22–25
-

Summary Reflection
Churches often recognize leadership gaps but avoid addressing them due to fear, conflict avoidance, or attachment to familiar structures.

Discussion Questions
1. What leadership challenges are visible but unaddressed in our church?
2. How does fear influence leadership decisions?
3. Where does avoidance show up in our culture?

Leadership Reflection
What conversations have I been delaying that faithfulness requires?

Action Step
Name one leadership issue that needs honest discussion and schedule time to address it.

CHAPTER 4 STUDY

Building Intergenerational Leadership Pathways

Key Theme
Leadership training must be intentional, not accidental.

Scripture Focus
- Ephesians 4:11–16
- Titus 2:1–8

Summary Reflection
Healthy churches create pathways for growth, training, and responsibility. Leadership development happens best when expectations are clear and relationships are strong.

Discussion Questions
1. What leadership pathways currently exist in our church?
2. Who has access to leadership development and who does not?
3. How can structure serve formation rather than control?

Leadership Reflection
How accessible is leadership development in our church?

Action Step
Design one clear pathway for emerging leaders to grow in responsibility.

CHAPTER 5 STUDY

Generations in Dialogue: From Tension to Trust

Key Theme
Trust grows through listening, not assumption.

Scripture Focus
- James 1:19
- Romans 12:3–8

Summary Reflection
Generational tension often stems from miscommunication and unspoken expectations. Trust is built when leaders commit to listening across difference.

Discussion Questions
1. Where do generations talk past each other in our church?
2. How does silence contribute to misunderstanding?
3. What would change if listening were treated as a leadership discipline?

Leadership Reflection
When was the last time I truly listened to someone from a different generation?

Action Step
Create a structured intergenerational listening session within the next quarter.

CHAPTER 6 STUDY

Generational Leadership and the Mission of the Church

Key Theme
Leadership renewal strengthens mission.

Scripture Focus
- Matthew 28:18–20
- Acts 2:42–47

Summary Reflection
Mission thrives when leadership is shared and renewed. When leadership stagnates, mission narrows.

Discussion Questions
1. How does leadership continuity impact our church's mission?
2. Where does leadership structure support or hinder outreach?
3. How can generational leadership expand witness?

Leadership Reflection
How does my leadership posture support the church's mission?

Action Step
Align leadership development efforts with missional priorities.

CHAPTER 7 STUDY

Faithful Stewards of What We Have Received

Key Theme
Faithfulness is measured by what we entrust forward.

Scripture Focus
- 1 Corinthians 4:1–2
- Psalm 145:4

Summary Reflection
Leadership stewardship requires courage, release, and trust in God's ongoing work across generations.

Discussion Questions
1. What has God entrusted to our church?
2. What might we be holding too tightly?
3. How do we prepare leaders beyond our own tenure?

Leadership Reflection
What does faithful release look like in my current season?

Action Step
Identify one leadership responsibility to intentionally share or entrust this year.

FINAL GROUP REFLECTION

Closing Questions
- How has your understanding of leadership changed?
- What commitments is God calling you to make?
- How can your church steward faith across generations more faithfully?

Closing Prayer
Invite participants to pray for humility, courage, and trust in God's work beyond the present moment.

Made in the USA
Coppell, TX
15 February 2026

71453209R00079